'This highly practical guide for therapists and interpreters provides a timely set of tips and guidelines based on years of experience delivering interpreter-mediated therapy. It addresses the needs and the anxieties of therapists and interpreters working together for the best possible outcomes for clients. The authors challenge the myth that interpreter-mediated therapy involves a loss and a reduction in emotional connection and depth. They provide significant examples from their own model of collaborative practice which has enhanced their ability to relate, provide psychological safety and containment and reach clients who are in great distress. This book is essential reading for any practitioner who wants to ensure that their practice is inclusive of multilingual populations and that it is delivered on the principles of linguistic justice.'

Dr Beverley Costa, CEO and Clinical Director of Mothertongue multi-ethnic counselling service www.mothertongue.org.uk

'This concise and easily accessible book written specifically for counsellors and psychotherapists is a useful addition to the literature and should be very helpful to counsellors and psychotherapists.'

Professor Rachel Tribe, Professor of Applied Psychology, School of Psychology, University of East London

Working with Interpreters in Psychological Therapy

This book is a practical and helpful guide for therapists that outlines best practice in working with interpreters. It provides an accessible tool for therapists working in a range of settings from small unfunded therapy teams in the voluntary sector to primary care work.

Working with Interpreters in Psychological Therapy has been written collaboratively by a therapist and an interpreter working in the refugee sector. The writers reflect upon how therapists can manage some of the complex dynamics that can occur in the triadic relationship and explore how the presence of an interpreter can bring additional psychological benefits to clients.

This book is essential reading for therapists working in cross-cultural settings, as well as the organizations in which they work.

Jude Boyles is a BACP Senior Accredited Psychological Therapist. She has been practising as a therapist for the last 24 years. Prior to qualifying, Jude worked within the women's movement in a Rape Crisis Centre and in Women's Aid refuges. Jude qualified as a therapist and worked in a mental health crisis service for 11 years, before establishing the Freedom from Torture North West Centre in Manchester. Jude has carried a caseload of torture survivors and managed the North West centre for the last 14 years.

Nathalie Talbot used to be a bilingual assistant at the Ethnic Diversity Service in Stockport, helping refugee children in primary schools. She is currently teaching the Ascentis Level 3 course in Community Interpreting. Nathalie has worked as an interpreter and trainer with Freedom from Torture North West since 2003.

Routledge Focus on Mental Health

Routledge Focus on Mental Health presents short books on current topics, linking in with cutting-edge research and practice.

Titles in the series:

Working with Interpreters in Psychological Therapy
The Right To Be Understood
Jude Boyles and Nathalie Talbot

Rational Emotive Behaviour Therapy
A Newcomer's Guide
Walter J. Matweychuk and Windy Dryden

Working with Interpreters in Psychological Therapy

The Right To Be Understood

Jude Boyles and Nathalie Talbot

Routledge
Taylor & Francis Group
LONDON AND NEW YORK

First published 2017
by Routledge
2 Park Square, Milton Park, Abingdon, Oxon OX14 4RN

and by Routledge
711 Third Avenue, New York, NY 10017

Routledge is an imprint of the Taylor & Francis Group, an informa business

British Library Cataloguing-in-Publication Data
A catalogue record for this book is available from the British Library

Library of Congress Cataloging-in-Publication Data
A catalog record for this book has been requested

ISBN: 978-1-138-22290-8 (hbk)
ISBN: 978-1-315-27215-3 (ebk)

Typeset in Times New Roman
by Apex CoVantage, LLC

Contents

Preface

We have wanted to write this book for some time. We have worked alongside each other for the last 14 years in psychological therapy and as trainers of both interpreters and therapists.

Our training delivery has aimed to develop the skills of interpreters to practice in a psychological therapy setting and our work with therapists has aimed to teach good practice working alongside interpreters. We have endeavoured to encourage therapists to explore how best to support interpreters to enhance the therapy and the development of the therapeutic relationship between therapist and client.

Much of what is written about working with interpreters in therapy examines the challenges of the three-way relationship, rather than explores how it might impact positively on the client, especially in therapy with refugees. As practitioners who work in the human rights field, we have substantial experience of the triad impacting positively on the therapeutic endeavour and on therapeutic work with refugees in particular.

Jude is an integrative therapist who has worked with interpreters in both statutory and third-sector settings for the last 18 years. Her first experience of working with interpreters was when establishing a Deaf People's Crisis Service in the statutory mental health sector alongside the local deaf community. A local British Sign Language Service (BSL) was engaged to enable deaf people to have the choice of being supported by an individual from the deaf community or with a therapist and BSL interpreter.

Jude then began working with survivors of conflict from Kosovo alongside a small number of Kosovan and Albanian interpreters in Leeds in 1998. Following the Asylum and Immigration Act in 1999, large numbers of people seeking asylum were dispersed to the West Yorkshire area, and work with interpreters from a wide range of countries became a significant part of the Crisis Centre's caseload.

In 2003, Jude established the first Freedom from Torture rehabilitation centre outside of London and the south-east of England. The centre offers a rehabilitation service to survivors of torture, almost all of whom are seeking asylum in the UK, or are refugees. As part of the development of the service, Jude trained up a team of therapists and interpreters to practice together to provide psychological therapies to refugee survivors of torture in the region. Part of Jude's and her team's work in both the statutory and third sector has been training and supervising practitioners working in a wide range of settings to practice effectively with interpreters in the therapeutic context.

Nathalie was born in the Ivory Coast, West Africa, where she began her education in a multicultural environment. In 1969, in the capital, Abidjan, she witnessed the students' uprising against the autocratic regime and the subsequent repression by the military. In 1982, she completed in Paris a master's degree in techniques of translation, English, and Russian, focusing on the theories of Mikhail Bakhtin, the semiotician and philosopher of human communication who inspired many Russian scholars and psychologists (1981).

Nathalie now lives in the UK. For the last 17 years, she has worked at the Ethnic Diversity Service in Greater Manchester as a bilingual assistant, helping refugee children who have fled from war zones in their acquisition of English in primary schools, and as an interpreter. She is currently teaching the Ascentis Level 3 course in community interpreting. She identified a growing need for more specialized training and designed two modules: on interpreting in a mental health setting, and on telephone interpreting.

Nathalie is a freelance interpreter/trainer, and has worked with Freedom from Torture North West since 2003.

This book shares the good practice learnt across the variety of settings that Jude and Nathalie have worked in and owes much to the refugee community in helping us define good practice.

In the current setting in which we offer therapy, almost all support is delivered alongside an interpreter. There is the structure in place to offer a highly trained and internally supervised interpreter, and interpreters have their own room in the building and are an intrinsic part of the makeup of the professional team.

We know that most therapists will not have access to a small cohort of highly trained interpreters and instead will be working with an interpreting agency, or accessing a bank of freelance interpreters. These interpreters may not have had specialist training in working within mental health and therapy settings, and may not have access to supervision. Most will not be prepared for the intensity of the material explored in the therapy context.

We hope this book provides guidance to therapists working in such settings and enables them to deliver the best practice possible in whatever context in which they are practising.

We will outline good practice as we see it, but also share our understanding of how to apply this approach when therapists are in situations that have less structured support for interpreters and there is little control of which interpreter is booked and through what agency.

We share our learning from some of the challenges we have encountered within our combined years of working in a range of settings and also explore some of the complex dynamics that can occur in the triad. We examine what support and supervision should be put in place for interpreters and how therapists might prepare and debrief interpreters they are working with.

Fourteen years on, we have arrived at a place where we are co-workers. When we work together, it is a partnership that aims to achieve the best service possible for our clients. It is collaborative and involves debate and discussion as we reflect together on the therapy delivered. Issues of power are named in the work, and shifting alliances in the triad explored.

Nathalie is fully present to our clients and to the therapists she works with. Her hunches, reflections, linguistic clues and understanding of syntax when it is being distorted are sought after, and add depth to our understanding of the impact of past events and current stressors on our clients.

In the book, we use the term *refugees* to describe both individuals seeking asylum in the UK and those granted asylum. In legal terms, a person who has asked for asylum in the UK and is waiting for a decision is described as a person/s seeking asylum. We have not used the term 'asylum seeker', due to its negative connotations. A refugee is an individual who has received a positive decision on his or her claim for asylum.

The case studies used throughout the book are fictional, except those given during Jude's work at a crisis service in Leeds. The fictional case studies are drawn from our combined years of working together across a range of different therapeutic settings.

Acknowledgements

We would like to thank those clients we have worked with in our respective positions of therapist and interpreter, as well as the therapists and interpreters who have helped us shape our practice.

Introduction

One of the most significant barriers to individuals whose first language is not English in accessing talking therapies is the limited access to bilingual therapists working within therapy services, but also a reluctance by therapists to work with interpreters. 'Language has been identified as a key barrier to accessing services and maintaining effective communication' (Smith, 2008: 21). In the same article, Smith cites a study whereby 37% of services offering mental health support to ethnic minority groups did not provide access to interpreters (Wilson, 2002).

No matter how diverse a therapy team is in terms of bilingual staff, there will always be a need for the use of interpreters in therapy. In most parts of the UK, people seeking asylum and refugees are accommodated in our communities and, given their experiences of war, gender-based abuses, torture and persecution, we can expect and hope that these individuals will be referred to psychological therapy services in both the third and statutory sectors. In addition, there are migrants who come to the UK to study, work or join families.

'Loss of language refers not to the literal loss of the ability to speak, but to the loss of opportunity to assert and exercise one's rights in exile, particularly when the dominant language is one with which the refugee person is unfamiliar' (Patel, 2003: 220).

It is almost impossible to give an accurate figure to reflect the diversity of languages now spoken in the UK. There is no single data collection site for the analysis of international migration, as ICAR outline in its report 'Mapping Refugee and Migrant Communities in the UK' (2010). Accessing data on those who seek international protection in the UK is challenging enough, but data on refugee populations is more difficult as those individuals and their families are mainstreamed into services once granted status.

What we do know is that in order for therapy services in both the third and statutory sectors to be accessible to refugee, migrant and non-English speaking communities, therapists will need to become trained and confident in working with interpreters. 'If culturally appropriate and accessible services are to be offered, interpreters will be required to share their skills and expertise with psychological services and they should be valued accordingly' (Tribe, 2007: 161, no 4).

This book focuses on working with interpreters in therapy who interpret for both therapist and client, and are professional team members. It does not examine or reflect on the role of bilingual link workers, or bilingual practitioners who also have a crucial role within mental health service provision.

Despite the reluctance to introduce a third person into the room, therapists can educate themselves on good practice in working alongside interpreters and develop their skills and confidence in working in a triad. If therapy services do not equip therapists to work effectively alongside interpreters, or non-qualified and unsupported interpreters are engaged, we risk what Van Parijs refers to as linguistic injustice in our therapy delivery, in that those who do not speak English are denied the right to be understood and influence (2004).

This book aims to provide a practical guide to good practice, based on our combined experience as a therapist and an interpreter and tutor. The guidance on good practice is applicable across all settings but can be more challenging to apply if therapists are in a setting where an agency is used and interpreters booked without any control or choice on behalf of the therapist. If the interpreters are not supervised or have had no access to training on mental health and therapeutic approaches, this challenge is likely to be amplified.

However, we believe that in any therapeutic setting, it is still possible for a therapist to apply many of the approaches explained in this book – that is, preparing the interpreter for therapy, outlining expectations and providing support after the session.

It is our experience that the presence of the interpreter can enhance an individual's recovery and add therapeutic benefit, rather than inhibit the development of a strong therapeutic alliance between the therapist and client. We have worked with interpreters alongside therapists from a wide range of disciplines and models, from cognitive behavioural therapy and eye movement desensitization reprocessing (EMDR) to humanistic approaches, gestalt or psychodynamic therapies. We have come to the conclusion that there is no particular model or discipline that limits the beneficial impact of having an interpreter in the room.

The anxiety for most therapists relates to how the impact of an interpreter might impede the development of the therapeutic relationship. All therapy is relational and the core task when client and therapist both meet is the development of a trusting therapeutic alliance. If there is another person in the room, therapists express concern that the relationship is affected, or psychological contact is blocked by the 'other' and they feel uncomfortable and unable to build an alliance. Therapists worry that their words and approach will not be truly transmitted to the client. They are worried that their challenges are softened to make them culturally accessible, or their gentle reflections become statements of fact or challenges. They fear that the client is naturally drawn to the interpreter and they can begin to feel like an outsider in the room, with the interpreter holding all the power.

The interpreter can feel overwhelmed and confused at the way in which the therapist is practising and alarmed at the material shared by the client and the depth of distress expressed. They may experience discomfort or unease when the therapist fails to understand the cultural nuances of a client's narrative, or be embarrassed by the silences. They may wonder why particular questions are being asked. Interpreters may struggle to translate all that is being said when the therapist leaves the client to speak in long streams, and they are left with the delicate task of interrupting the client, taking power and shouldering more responsibility than they are used to.

The client may feel naturally drawn to the interpreter and even believe that they have found someone they are able to connect with and who understands their frame of reference. In contrast, they may worry about confidentiality and what might be shared in the community. They feel concern that the interpreter may judge or pity them or wonder whether the interpreter shares their political beliefs or is from an opposition party.

The potential for confusion and misunderstanding can be significant, but much can be done to avoid some of these unhelpful dynamics with a proactive approach to working with interpreters and preparation of both the interpreter and therapist.

Rachel Tribe, in an article that explores the three-way relationship in therapeutic work with interpreters, and in other papers, argues that therapeutic work with interpreters can be viewed more negatively than is warranted: 'the inherent advantages of this way of engaging with the non-English speaking client have been minimised and ignored' (Tribe, 2009: 13).

A key theme we have consistently noted throughout our work together is the importance of giving choice to the client. We can make assumptions that an individual would prefer a bilingual therapist, or want to speak in a particular language, usually their mother tongue. In reality, clients have complex reasons that are multilayered as to what language they would like to work in, and whether their first or tribal tongue is chosen, or their second language.

Clients may want an interpreter from their own country and sometimes even region, and at other times request that the interpreter comes from a different country. We cannot know what might make a client feel safer, but we can ask and negotiate. What we do know is that the interpreter can either block the helpfulness of therapy and impact negatively on the therapeutic alliance or be another affirming and supportive relationship that sits gently alongside the core relationship of the therapist and the client.

There has been little research on the impact of an interpreter on therapeutic work with traumatized survivors of torture, the field we currently work in. One study in East London of the use of cognitive behavioural therapy (CBT) to treat traumatized refugees found that refugees receiving CBT with and without an interpreter did not differ in treatment outcomes (D'Ardenne et al., 2007).

Most interpreters, regardless of whether they are trained and experienced in working in a mental health setting, will be eager to demonstrate that they can deliver, but will expect direction and information in order to meet the therapist's expectations. If this energy or drive is not channelled positively, interpreters may align themselves with the client, protecting him or her from the painful work of therapy.

Interpreters are used to working in isolation, without any support from their agency, but they may also be anxious or lacking in confidence in this new area of work. If interpreters do not receive guidance or understanding from the practitioner in this sensitive and unfamiliar setting, they may not be able to practice appropriately and may unwillingly obstruct the process of therapy or slow down the development of the therapeutic alliance.

1 Preparatory work and booking an interpreter for the first time

If a therapy service is new to working with interpreters, and has some choice in which interpreting agency can be approached, it can be useful to seek advice from other therapy services working with refugees or non-English speaking communities. There are often many interpreting and translation services in any given area, but some may not use qualified interpreters. Try to approach an agency that is trusted in the therapy sector. Some third-sector therapy services may have their own bank of qualified freelance interpreters, and may be willing to share their details.

It can be useful to set up a meeting with the interpreting agency, and be prepared to ask some questions about their processes to ensure the safety of clients. The differences between a professional interpreter and a non-qualified interpreter are significant.

Once an agency has been identified, it can be very helpful as a start to offer interested interpreters a training session on the work of the therapeutic service, outlining the therapeutic approach and which client groups are supported. Clarity on whether the work is long-term or brief is an important theme to cover on the training as long-term therapy can impact differently on the interpreter. Miller et al. in their study noted how the long-term nature of refugee work alongside the intense material explored sets interpreting with refugees apart from interpreting in other settings (2005). Services might offer long-term therapeutic work specifically with refugee populations, young people and/or families, or survivors of sexual violence, or it may be a generic service to all communities, offering mostly short-term interventions within a primary care counselling setting.

Delivering training can both equip and prepare the interpreting team engaged, but also gives a clear message to interpreters that therapists are keen to work alongside them, value their skills and want the interpreting team to be fully aware of the type of work they will be engaging in and its potential impact. Outline what is expected as well as what the therapists can offer interpreters: a pre-briefing, a debriefing and additional support and supervision if required.

If the therapy team is working with trauma or is a crisis service, describe the types of difficulties interpreters can expect to work with. Most therapeutic work involves suicide risk assessments, and so providing some teaching on the nature of suicide risk is always helpful. Our experience shows us that without specific training on trauma, interpreters seem at greater risk of vicarious trauma. If the service works with perpetrators of violence, such as in a men's prison setting, ensure that there are male interpreters available and that the interpreting team is informed and given a choice about working in this field.

Providing a full day's training might not be possible in some settings, but at the very least, ensure that there is a meeting between the interpreting and therapy teams. This can be a productive first step to building good working relationships. Without this introduction and an exchange of guidelines and expectations, there can be misunderstandings that impact directly on clients.

At the end of each section we have included a set of brief guidelines in bullet point form that follow the narrative. Interpreting agencies will have their own code of practice and qualified interpreters will also have the ethical framework and code of practice of their professional body.

Establishing that both interpreters and therapists have a senior manager to approach in both services when there are problems is crucial. Inevitably there will be occasions when the interpreter is unhappy at the conduct or approach of the therapist, or the therapist may need to share concerns with the interpreting service manager about an interpreter's English (or first language) not being sophisticated enough for psychological therapy. Either way, a pathway to address concerns from both sides is needed.

Once a therapy service has established that the agency has engaged a qualified interpreting team, booking arrangements will need to be discussed.

'The right to understand and receive appropriate communication support is a civil right and fundamental to an inclusive and democratic society that seeks to ensure that it provides for the needs of all its citizens' (Scottish Translation, Interpreting and Communication Forum, 2004: 6).

It almost goes without saying that the therapist should aim to use the same interpreter throughout the therapeutic contract. This need for continuity should be made explicit to the agency to ensure that an interpreter who is due to take a long break, or who has limited availability, is not booked for an assessment. Once the therapist has identified an interpreter he or she is happy to work with, the interpreter can be named and pre-booked in advance for the duration of therapy. Ask the agency not to send another interpreter if, for any reason, the usual interpreter is not available, and to contact the therapy service first.

Therapists should state the gender/language and dialect of the interpreter required when booking and also state the country of origin and/or region if this is important for the client. It is both acceptable and client-centred to be very specific when booking a new interpreter, to avoid communication difficulties in the first session. Assessment sessions are important in terms of engagement between client and therapist and booking the most appropriate interpreter for the session is a priority. Poor communication can significantly impact on the depth of the work that can be achieved and so it is acceptable for example to ask for an *Iraqi male – Arabic interpreter* or *Swahili (Democratic Republic of Congo [DRC]) female interpreter*.

It is important never to assume that the stated language on the referral information is the preferred language of the client for therapy. We have discovered that the choice of language in therapy is far more nuanced than the simple 'first language good, other languages bad' formula (Costa, 2011: 20). There are frequent assumptions about what language an individual speaks and prefers, and so, where possible, ask prior to booking. If the language/dialect or the gender fit is not appropriate, the therapist can use the first session as an opportunity to explore what language is preferred and arrange this for the follow-up session. Bear in mind that stated nationality does not necessarily tell you what language is best to use in therapy.

It is also a good idea to find out if there are differences in dialects within a language – for example, the lingua franca Swahili is not the same spoken in Kenya as it is in Uganda and Eastern DRC; Pashto from Afghanistan and Pashto from Pakistan are dissimilar. Kurdish is a very complex language with three distinctive dialect groups: Sorani, Kumanji and Pehlewani. A guide to languages by country can be found at the website www.ethnologue.com.

Clients may choose to work in a second or third language as it distances them from traumatic experiences. However, they may find themselves involuntarily returning to their mother tongue at times of distress or despair or when processing traumatic memories. For individuals who have been tortured and/or experienced other forms of abuse, the sound of their own language may trigger traumatic memories, and so survivors might choose to have an interpreter who speaks their second or third language. However, many individuals are able to express their true feelings only in a first or second language. Particular words, phrases and emphases convey meaning within any cultural framework and are an intrinsic part of expression.

Within the services we have worked in, we have observed that on most occasions, female clients prefer a female interpreter, and within the setting we work in together now, with refugee survivors of torture, a female interpreter is always booked for female survivors. 'The experience or threat of violence affects boundaries of wealth, race and culture. In the home and in the community, in times of war and peace, women are beaten, raped, mutilated, and killed with impunity' (Amnesty International, 2006).

Therapists should give some thought to the setting where therapy is being delivered. Many interpreters are expected to sit in the waiting area with clients they are due to interpret for. It is preferable to provide a separate space from clients so that interpreters can prepare themselves for the session, and can recover afterwards if needed. A separate space also protects an interpreter from clients approaching them to ask questions, request translation of a letter or a medication information leaflet or try to form a social relationship. If there is no separate waiting area, then discussions with the interpreter in the pre-briefing about how the interpreter might manage these encounters will be important. Request that the interpreter gently and politely ask the client to wait to talk until the session, outlining that the interpreter must not attempt to translate or advocate for the client in any way. A reminder to not give their telephone number to a client may also be appropriate.

A further issue to be considered at booking stage is whether the interpreter is known to the client from another professional setting, or from within the community. It is our experience that if possible, it is best to use interpreters in therapy who have not interpreted for the client in other settings in order to preserve the unique and separate space of therapy. With rare languages or in situations when the client has requested a particular interpreter, the therapist may have to use an interpreter who has an established relationship with the client and prior knowledge of his or her situation and difficulties. This can create a complex dynamic, but if this is the only available triad, then it still is possible to make it work, if handled thoughtfully. We will explore how such dynamics can be managed later in the book.

On no occasion in therapy is it ever ethical or acceptable to use an interpreter who is a relative, friend or close community contact of the client in therapy. Children should never be used to interpret.

For confidentiality reasons, the name of the client is not stated at the booking stage, but interpreters should be asked to disclose immediately when they arrive at a session if the client is known to them. They do not have to give any detailed information of the setting/s in which they have met the client but have to ensure that the therapist and client are comfortable to continue with the session. If it is appropriate to progress – that is, the interpreter has met the client only in another professional setting and does not have close links – it is vital that the confidentiality policy of both the therapist and interpreter is fully outlined at the start of the appointment. The client should also be informed that it is his or her right to ask for another interpreter. Therapists can also explain the reasons why a relative or a community advocate is not suitable for therapy.

Interpreting is a highly skilled profession but appropriate credentials are not always required by translation and interpreting agencies. Unfortunately, for rare languages, therapists may be dependent on non-qualified interpreters. In many cases, interpreters have been added to an agency's books simply because they had a UK university qualification, or have lived in the UK for 20 years and proved fluent in English, or were the only ones to speak a rare language in the region. Without training, interpreters will not have been language-tested or have had verified listening skills and an understanding of various interpreting techniques. They may also have an insufficient knowledge of terminology in their first language, as they would have been assessed mainly in English.

Many agencies claim that they provide an online training and induction but this may prove to be untrue or just inadequate. It takes up to eight weeks to complete a Disclosure and Barring (DBS or Disclosure Scotland) check; however, interpreters can be offered assignments before being thoroughly checked.

In 2012, a Russian linguist who had not trained as an interpreter decided to test the system and registered his cat Masha for the very rare Cat language. This was accepted without any valid qualifications or DBS check. This same linguist also registered online and on his mobile application was offered work straightaway (BBC News, 2012).

Questions for the interpreting agency:

- Are the interpreters qualified and to what standard? Request that interpreters have a Diploma in Public Service Interpreting (DPSI) or equivalent, such as Ascentis Level 3 course in community interpreting or Chartered Institute of Linguists (CIOL) Diploma.
- Are the interpreters required to undertake a regular DBS check (Disclosure and Barring Service, or in Scotland, Disclosure Scotland) and are references taken up prior to acceptance by the agency? The DBS should be enhanced.
- Do members of the interpreting team also work for the Home Office? It is likely that individuals seeking asylum in the UK will not feel safe with an interpreter working alongside decision makers within the asylum process.
- Ask for a copy of the Code of Practice and/or Code of Conduct of the interpreting agency, which should include themes such as confidentiality and impartiality.
- Ask what languages are offered, and whether there are male and female interpreters in the team for the languages most frequently required in the service.

- Ask for the booking process, and request that when a named interpreter is booked, this interpreter is not replaced by another if she or he becomes unavailable.
- Ask what internal training has been provided to the interpreting team.
- Ask what supervision arrangements are in place. There may be none, but it is important for therapists to know what support the interpreting agency provides as this will inevitably lead to therapists being required to provide ongoing supervision and support for interpreters.
- Ask which interpreters have experience of working within psychological therapy and mental health settings and request for these to be booked where possible.
- Ask that any interpreters arriving for an interpreting booking at the therapy agency disclose immediately to the therapist if the client is known to them in any capacity, either professionally (they do not need to disclose how) or personally.

Guidelines once an interpreting agency/freelance team has been engaged:

- Provide training to the therapy team on good practice in working with interpreters as well as outlining the role of the interpreter.
- Train and brief the team of interpreters who have experience of/or are committed to working in psychological therapy on the work of the service.
- Agree that when an interpreter is booked for a new client or therapist, he or she is offered a half hour of pre-briefing with the therapist.
- Give some consideration as to where interpreters wait for clients so interpreters are protected from being approached by clients seeking advice or social contact.
- Establish clear booking arrangements and ensure the agency will fulfil your requests in terms of language and dialect/gender and availability of interpreter on a regular basis. This is to ensure you can provide consistency of interpreter for the client.
- Establish clear lines of communication between both the therapy and interpreting agency so any concerns can be addressed speedily to reduce the impact on clients.

2 The role of an interpreter

From a social constructionist approach, Mudarikiri writes that 'relationships between people can be thought about as existing within the web of meanings that are created by language' (2003: 183). The therapist, interpreter and client are in a relationship together and how they communicate and understand each other is determined by the context in which the dialogues are taking place.

Language is complex and the task of linguistic interpretation is a highly challenging process, as it involves not just words but also interpreting the meaning behind what is being said. 'Each different language makes particular meanings possible and allows us to experience certain aspects of ourselves' (Mudarikiri, 2003: 183).

It is usually not possible to simply translate from one language to another. 'The interpreter has the unenviable task of rendering a meaningful translation that reflects all the levels at which communication is taking place' (Mudarikiri, 2003: 189). Meanings may be coded or there may not be a word for a concept that is part of the cultural landscape of a country, such as the language of trauma prevalent in the UK. Alongside this, how we understand health, express distress and seek help varies from culture to culture. 'Interpreting requires more than just word for word translation, and advances meaning in the fullest linguistic and cultural sense, so that two people can understand each other beyond their words' (Raval, 2003: 16).

It is often assumed that only interpreters require training on the role of therapy, but our experience is that therapists frequently misunderstand the role of the interpreter or do not appreciate the complexity and skills of the profession. Delivering training for therapists on the interpreter's role is crucial in creating a working alliance between practitioners where interpreters feel that their skills are understood and valued.

Therapists do not always manage the dynamic in the triad well *because* of a lack of understanding of the role, as well as other anxieties about having a third person in the room and the exposure of having a witness to their work.

Many interpreters working within non-specialist settings may not practice skilfully, with an awareness of the potential impact of their presence on a client. However, if therapists are aware of what constitutes good practice, they are much more likely to be clear with the interpreter about what they require and be confident enough to challenge when the interpreter is not working appropriately.

The task of interpreting is highly skilled. The role carries significant responsibility and requires high levels of concentration, as well as sensitivity to a wide range of settings. The interpreter's role is to convey the meaning of everything that is said in an exchange between two people who do not share the same language. Interpreters need to be proficient in their own language/s and in English (in most settings in the UK). They must endeavour to be accurate and translate all that is said from an impartial position. Impartiality is emphasized in the profession, but it must be remembered that interpreters will process the narrative through their own subjective experiences, and so it is inevitable that the material may be influenced at times by their own knowledge and life history. Professional and ethical interpreters will reflect on this and share concerns with the therapist when they become aware of changing the emphasis, or missing out words or phrases in their work.

Interpreters are expected to reflect the tone of both individuals, as well as subtly render hesitations, pauses and stammers. This is a more intimate and delicate process. Experienced interpreters may be concerned about whether the client understands why a speech impediment is being gently repeated or indicated, or why their narrative is being translated verbatim with its natural clumsiness and imperfections. This can feel uncomfortable to the interpreter and can be misunderstood by a client as a lack of consideration. Clients may feel humiliated to hear their struggle for words interpreted, and wish the interpreter would use their most eloquent English. However, many clients are reassured by the attention to accuracy. It is good practice to review the interpreting arrangement as therapy progresses.

On one occasion, a client said that they knew the interpreter was thorough and trustworthy because they could hear their own hesitations and stammer being keyed in English. Far from being disempowered by this observation, the client was confident that their account was listened to with respect. As they were doing their best at learning English and understanding how to cross the emotional barrier, they were also able to recognize how their feelings could be put in another language, using their pauses and hesitations, and occasional stammer as cues to rebuild their narrative. This comment was met with relief and comforted the interpreter in their practice with other clients.

Interpreters should be aware of the subtlety of the emotional content of what is expressed, ensuring they capture the emphasis in an individual's narrative. They should be attentive to the grammatical construction within the languages they are fluent in and acknowledge when a word has several meanings. Skilled and experienced interpreters may also find themselves naturally reflecting the body language of non-English speakers to make their interpretation as objective as possible. In some Arabic cultures, it would not be appropriate for an interpreter to mimic the body language of some clients, as this may make the individual feel conspicuous or uncomfortable, and be understood as a lack of respect. On such occasions, a more neutral attitude will then be favoured.

Interpreters are expected to conduct themselves in a professional manner, and be non-judgemental and discreet in their approach, regardless of their own belief systems, or the attitudes of the client or therapist towards them. Interpreters should interpret all that is said in the way that it is said. If interpreters do not understand some of the meaning, they should seek clarification and ensure that both individuals are aware that they need to check what has been said to translate it accurately. The interpreter should not voice an opinion during an appointment, or make comments on any aspect of the dialogue. The interpreter should not interrupt either the client or practitioner.

The interpreter is not a cultural expert, or in the role of a bilingual link worker, or advocate. Interpreters should not provide any explanations, or intervene if they are feeling uncomfortable with aspects of the dialogue. Interpreters can say if they feel that there has been a misunderstanding.

Interpreters do have a role in sharing their cultural understanding in the debriefing session, and it is helpful if this includes the meaning of non-verbal communication observed during the session, as well as the nuances of the language and dialect used. We would always advise caution as there are risks in a therapist using a bilingual colleague as a cultural broker. Interpreters can suggest clues but still need to appreciate their cultural experience might differ from a client's. Interpreters should never give an opinion on whether the client has lived or was born in a particular country or region; they are also not country experts.

Interpreters must observe confidentiality at all times, and are expected not to disclose any information to a third party. They should not share information known about a client from a different setting to a therapist. Agency interpreters do not share information with either interpreting colleagues or their agency. Interpreters are expected to hold considerable amounts of personal information.

Interpreters who have worked with one member of a couple should disclose this to the therapist, and in most cases it would not be appropriate for an interpreter to work with both members of a couple seeing different therapists within any setting. In the context of domestic violence, particular care should be taken to protect interpreters working with the family member at risk. The perpetrator of violence may pose a danger to the safety of the interpreter, who they see as having crucial information about the whereabouts of the partner or holding disclosures the survivor has made to his or her therapist. In settings where women are seeking therapy following male violence, being able to offer a female therapist and interpreter is vital. Interpreters working in such settings would benefit from training on the nature of domestic violence, with particular emphasis on confidentiality and keeping themselves safe.

Interpreters, like therapists, should not have personal relationships with clients, or initiate informal contact with clients when they meet an individual away from the professional setting. Therapists are members of or are accredited or registered with professional bodies that provide guidance on when it might be acceptable to have any form of social relationship with an ex-client, such as two years after therapy has ended. No such guidance is provided to interpreters. It may be useful for the therapy agency to provide guidance on this issue in their agreement with the agency if it is not included in the interpreting agency's code of practice.

Interpreters who are experienced in working alongside therapists will be sensitive to the fact that the client may engage with them first, and will develop skill in establishing trust with clients, and then reducing eye contact to facilitate engagement between client and therapist. The art of being discreet and conveying warmth and acceptance while translating is a sophisticated task and requires considerable focus.

There are two national bodies that have a recognized code of conduct that qualified interpreters adhere to, depending on their qualification/s or membership in the professional body.

In the UK, the Institute of Translation and Interpreting (ITI) has a code of professional conduct to which agencies and freelance interpreters can adhere to. The ITI is a membership organization and the professional body for qualified interpreters and translators. A full copy of the code can be found at the Institute. The National Register of Public Service Interpreters (NRPSI) also has a code of conduct, which sets out the professional conduct of the registrants on the NRPSI, and similarly covers themes such as professional conduct, ethics, confidentiality and working within one's competency. All place emphasis on impartiality.

There is also likely to be an additional code of conduct within the interpreting agency.

Mothertongue, a cross-cultural psychotherapy service in London, has produced a 'Code of Practice and Ethics for Interpreters and Practitioners in

Joint Work', which is available from www.mothertongue.org.uk. The British Psychological Society (BPS) has also published a set of guidelines: 'Working with Interpreters in Health Settings for Clinical Psychologists' (2008). These guidelines are due to be updated and are available from the BPS.

The following list reflects some of the core principles and values of the foregoing two interpreting and translation professional bodies, but has been written as a brief guide for therapists working with community language interpreters in therapy, and is therefore therapy-specific.

Code of conduct for interpreters in therapy:

- The interpreter's role is to interpret between two languages so that effective communication can take place. The NRPSI states that the interpreter 'shall interpret truly and faithfully what is uttered, without adding, omitting or changing anything'.
- Interpreters should speak in the first person.
- Simultaneous interpreting is generally felt not to be appropriate for a therapy setting.
- The interpreter should be felt by both the client and therapist as a discreet and gentle presence.
- Interpreters should reflect the tone, hesitations, emphasis and pauses within the dialogue between the therapist and client.
- Interpreters must retain the confidentiality of clients at all times, and across all settings in which they have had contact with a client. This duty of confidentiality persists beyond the completion of therapy.
- Interpreters should practice with integrity, and be punctual and honest.
- Interpreters should not accept gifts from clients. In the aforementioned professional codes, it does not prohibit the exchange of small gifts but therapy services often have a gift policy which interpreters should be made aware of.
- Interpreters are expected to decline work outside of their competence either linguistically or because of a lack of a specialized knowledge.
- Interpreters should take all reasonable steps to ensure clear communication between both individuals, including intervention to prevent misunderstanding.
- Interpreters should not volunteer any opinion on a client.
- Interpreters should be non-judgemental and let clients feel they can express themselves freely.
- Interpreters should not meet a client socially outside of their professional assignment. If they happen to meet each other within their community, boundaries should be maintained and/or a discreet greeting.

- Interpreters should respect silences in sessions and follow the pace set by the therapist.
- Interpreters should be transparent. If for any reason they are alone with the client, they should make it clear that they will disclose anything said to them directly to the therapist.
- Interpreters have the right to intervene, to seek clarification or to clarify any cultural misunderstanding. They should not volunteer any knowledge from other professional fields – that is, legal or housing.
- Interpreters should not touch clients, and need to maintain an appropriate physical distance.
- Interpreters should have empathy without expressing their personal feelings or losing composure. If they feel distressed or emotional, they can ask permission to leave the room during the session.

3 Briefing the interpreter

When a therapist and interpreter are meeting for the first time, we recommend a half hour pre-briefing. This session is an opportunity for the therapist to outline what he or she expects from the interpreter and to describe how he or she will approach the session and what the interpreter can expect in terms of support, briefing and debriefing.

In many settings interpreters are not briefed and enter sessions with a GP, therapist or other social care or health provider unaware of what to expect. Interpreters can feel unprepared and unprotected. Establishing how both will work together can be tremendously reassuring for an interpreter.

We have outlined the role of the interpreter and defined good practice. However, in circumstances where an interpreter has been booked who is not practising within this approach, the therapist may need to intervene almost immediately to ensure that the client is getting the best service possible. Interpreters may start to interpret simultaneously immediately when everyone is seated, or interpret in the third person. They may change the seating when they enter the room so they are sitting closer and in the eye-line of the client. Interpreters may introduce themselves to the client first, without being prompted by the therapist, and begin a casual conversation. Interpreters might hug or touch a client known to them. As a result, it is always advisable to state core good practice expectations in the pre-briefing to ensure interpreters do not enter the session as an advocate or take the lead once everyone is seated.

Many interpreters have not had the benefit of support and supervision and work alongside healthcare staff who have also had no training. This can inevitably lead to some interpreters assuming the role of advocate, and positioning themselves as experts on the client/s. They may make cultural observations or other interventions in session as they see themselves as a community or client representative, disempowering the client in the process. When a client produces a letter or a photograph, and hands it to them, they may take it and even look at it before passing it directly to the therapist.

It can sometimes be helpful to challenge the interpreter in the session if he or she is not working as agreed between you in the pre-briefing. There are risks in challenging in a first session together as it may embarrass a client or create unhelpful alliances in the triad. However, there is also a risk in letting poor interpretation go and the therapist may lose control of the session if he or she is not assertive and clear about what conduct is expected.

It is useful to give the client's name in the pre-briefing and describe the purpose of the appointment and how you intend to structure the session, as well as provide some background on the client. Feeling unsure of what to expect in any given appointment can be anxiety-provoking for interpreters, and might make them more likely to take control by default. Explain that the therapist will always take a break after 50 minutes to an hour as interpreters cannot be expected to concentrate for longer without the linguistic quality of their work being affected. Breaks also provide an opportunity to clarify any possible misunderstandings and ask questions.

Ask the interpreter to interpret all that is said by both client and therapist, to reflect your tone and emphasis and to speak in the first person. Ask the interpreter to have some eye contact in the beginning with the client, as trust is established. Reflect that it is hoped that as the relationships develop, the interpreter will reduce eye contact to a minimum so that eye contact is facilitated between the therapist and client.

Ask interpreters to let the therapist know if they are seeking clarification, and to relay hesitations, stammers and pauses where they can. Explain that it is the therapist who will manage the narrative, and ask interpreters not to interrupt the client. It is the therapist's role to manage the session, and pace the narrative if a client is speaking in long stretches. The therapist can reassure the interpreter that he or she will take the lead if a client is distressed, and even if it is culturally customary, to refrain from comforting a client who is distressed.

Interpreters may not understand the purpose of the questions asked by the therapist and this may block their ability to interpret with accuracy. They may be distracted with their own questions as they are unclear of the motives behind the therapist's responses. The interpreter might observe that the client is crying, but the therapist does not seem to be offering any reassurance or care. Interpreters might not comprehend why the therapist is asking the client questions that are causing such distress, and they might find this difficult to witness. Therapists will need to ask interpreters to trust the process of therapy as well as the practice of the therapist. Explain that there will be silences during the process and why that might be, and explore how they might behave if there are silences or long periods of distress.

If a therapist is assessing suicide risk or working with a very traumatized individual, outline how the assessment will be approached, and how aroused or distressed clients are supported. It can be frightening or shocking for interpreters when a client jumps up and has a panic attack, or suddenly moves and cowers in a corner of the room, and reverts to a different language. Describe what such responses are and what tools or approaches the therapist will engage in when these occur.

Ask interpreters not to touch the client, and if the client asks any direct questions of them, to simply interpret the question. Ask if interpreters have any concerns about the session and explain that they will debriefed after the session and, if they are experiencing impact or secondary traumatization, further support is available.

Interpreters may say in the pre-briefing when the issue of support is discussed that they are experienced and used to interpreting across a wide variety of settings. They may be unaware of the density of the counselling process, and of its repeated action. We have found that the very nature of the material explored in therapy and the depth of distress witnessed impact significantly on interpreters.

Experienced interpreters are often engaged by asylum lawyers and interpret detailed accounts of human rights abuses for witness statements. Despite their familiarity with the asylum field, interpreters may not be prepared for the painful expressions of grief, guilt and shame that take place week after week and sometimes over a long period of time in the process of therapy with refugees. Interpreters may be in denial of the impact, not recognizing that they are overwhelmed by the material, and resist acknowledgement of how they are affected for fear of being judged or found inadequate by the therapist. It is important for therapists to reassure interpreters that they will be impacted and their professionalism will not be put in question. Providing ongoing support must always be part of the role of the therapist when traumatic material is being explored.

Interpreters who are overwhelmed by the material can shut down in the session in order to manage their distress, which is likely to come across as distance or boredom to the client or therapist. Interpreters need to be an empathic and gentle presence. This can be a reassuring and helpful addition for the client in therapy when offered by both therapist and interpreter. If the interpreter is fully supported and contained, the interpreter can be fully present and involved, but remain separate enough to feel psychologically safe.

Reassure interpreters that they will neither be left in the room with the client nor be expected to answer direct questions. It is useful to discuss with interpreters what personal information they are comfortable with being disclosed, such as their country of origin.

Position the seating so that the therapist and client are sitting opposite each other, and the interpreter is to one side. This arrangement ensures that the client is encouraged to look at the therapist if there is eye contact. Once the session is underway, the therapist has no need to look at the interpreter but, of course, the client may choose to look at both throughout the session.

Briefing guidelines:

- Give the name of the client to the interpreter to ensure the client is not known in either a personal or professional capacity.
- Give brief information about the client, if known, such as country of origin, age and other relevant background and client history.
- Describe the therapeutic approach and what the session will look like. Explain how the therapist will introduce themselves and what is expected from the interpreter in terms of introductions. Agree who will outline the code of confidentiality for the interpreter.
- Outline what is expected from the interpreter: speak in the first person, reflect tone, have discreet presence and so forth.
- Explain that the therapist holds clinical responsibility for the session, manages the pacing and explores with the client the need to speak in small chunks – that is, two sentences at a time.
- Ask the interpreter to be mindful of what tense is being used by both the therapist and the client at all times, especially when working with traumatized individuals.
- Ask the interpreter not to touch a client, pass tissues or follow the client if a client jumps or moves in the clinical room.
- Ask the interpreter to respect and *sit with* silences.
- Reassure the interpreter that he or she will not be left alone in the room with a client.
- Reassure the interpreter that he or she will not have to answer direct personal questions and just to interpret a question if asked. Agree what can be shared.
- Ask the interpreter to follow the therapist's lead if a client becomes highly aroused or distressed.
- Ask the interpreter to pass any documents, photographs or mobile pictures or films to the therapist if given them in the course of a session by the client.
- If a letter needs to be translated, the therapist will read it out rather than pass the document to the interpreter to translate in full.
- Reassure and prepare the interpreter for clients who may show injuries or scars from assaults, torture or self-harm and outline how the therapist may respond. Interpreters should not have to look at injuries.

- Reassure interpreters that they will be debriefed after the session and that if they are distressed or feel overwhelmed, they can request a break and leave the room.
- It is useful to ask interpreters to manage their own responses, as it can be disturbing for a client if the interpreter gasps in shock, nods frequently or smiles/laughs before the comment has been translated to the therapist.
- Emphasize that it is a normal part of the process for the client to engage with the interpreter first, and the client may well have more eye contact with the interpreter at the beginning of therapy. Ask the interpreter to reduce eye contact as relationships develop, to facilitate eye contact between client and therapist.
- Explore how the interpreter will seek to clarify misunderstandings.
- Agree on a pause signal between you, as sometimes during an intense and fast-moving session, either the therapist or interpreter may need to stop the dialogue.
- Reiterate the importance of respect, empathy and being non-judgemental.

4 Good practice in working with interpreters in therapy

It is now widely accepted in the refugee therapy sector that whenever there is an interpreter present, there is a three-way relationship (Baker and Briggs, 1975). 'Each participant has a role to play, an agenda and set of expectations and assumptions of their own. Additionally, each has a relationship with the other – as well as a relationship as a three' (Smith, 2008: 22).

The interpreter has a relationship with both the therapist and the client and cannot be made invisible or reduced to 'just a voice'. Many writers in the field describe a triangular relationship with the distance between those present being the same. Tribe notes in her paper on exploring the three-way dynamic that the 'distance between the three participants is always in motion, shifting depending on the material being addressed' (2009: 15).

Most therapists are anxious about working with interpreters in therapy. Indeed, we have delivered training to many teams over the years who have said that it is not possible to work effectively with interpreters in a therapy setting and have studiously avoided it where they can! The process of interpretation does slow down the pace of therapy, but in many instances, this may be helpful. It enables more reflective time for the therapist and 'more space to gently stop the narrative and explore feelings and sensations' (Boyles et al., 2015: 14). In therapeutic work with survivors of torture, hearing a survivor's non-native language may make trauma work less overwhelming.

As a therapist, I remember feeling quite exposed in my first session with an interpreter. It was quite disconcerting to have a third person in the room and to start therapy with a client whose focus was on the interpreter rather than on me. Over the years I have grown to enjoy the collaborative element of having a third person in the room, and been tremendously moved by how much the additional presence of another caring practitioner can benefit the client. The client has a further witness to his or her history of abuse and the human rights commitment of the interpreter has been experienced as further validation for a survivor of abuse. 'Inevitably the interpreter is called upon to facilitate communication, not as a neutral linguist but as an active participant in the struggle against human rights abuses' (Patel, 2003: 222).

Judith Herman reflects that in therapy with survivors of political violence, whether gender-based abuse or torture and/or conflict, the therapist is called upon to bear witness to a crime and this involves being in solidarity with a survivor (1994). 'As such, the stance of non-neutrality can be interpreted as a political stance against human rights abuses' (Patel, 2003: 222).

In our work together as interpreter and therapist, we have been able to be explicit about our human rights commitment with our clients, and have seen the powerful impact this can have on recovery.

The process of the translation allows the therapist more time to think and reflect on interventions, and it can help pace a session with a traumatized individual. There is more space for psychological contact without words between the therapist and the client while the interpreter speaks. As a therapist, it can feel as if myself and the client are almost alone in the space for those moments. When a client has smiled for the first time, or makes a joke that we all laugh at, the intimacy and shared experience can be beneficial to a client, as are the dialogues across cultures as we endeavour to understand the meaning of a survivor's narrative.

A client recently reflected after I had sent him an audio recording of myself and our interpreter doing a relaxation exercise for him to listen to on his mobile phone before bed: '*your* voices helped me get to sleep quickly for the first time last night'.

When the therapist is from another culture, and his or her approach and demeanour is new or uncomfortable, the familiarity of the interpreter's language and presence can be containing and make therapy possible in the beginning. The gentle and warm presence of the interpreter can be felt as validating and reassuring to a client. When the trust in the therapist grows, the presence of two caring and supportive individuals being alongside an individual in pain can be tremendously affirming and significant. This is the case for many refugee clients living in exile, who ache for home and find themselves isolated and bewildered by a new culture and a confusing set of societal norms.

Following the pre-briefing, it can be helpful for therapists to introduce themselves to the client in the waiting room, separately from the interpreter. This facilitates engagement, but also sets a clear boundary in relation to the role of the interpreter as being for both client and therapist. When everyone is seated, it is almost always the case that the client is immediately drawn to the interpreter. Clients will understandably want to establish if they recognize the interpreter and try to read other cues that might indicate whether the interpreter is an individual to be trusted. This is a normal process and it is important to give the client space to make this assessment.

Therapists should introduce themselves and explain their role. It can facilitate trust if those first few interchanges illustrate to a client the calm and easy way the therapist and interpreter work together. Most clients will have had experiences of interpreters working less professionally, or even had the experience of an interpreter impacting negatively on their interview at the Home Office. Clients may have been in settings where the health professional addressed the interpreter throughout the consultation, or they could sense in a previous exchange that their narrative was not being transmitted accurately.

Therapists should introduce themselves first and then invite the interpreter to do the same. Each therapist will have his or her own approach to how to introduce and open a first session, as well as an organizational remit and assessment structure. The key thing to remember is to be aware that, for many clients, it can be anxiety-provoking to have an interpreter in the room. It is likely that they would distrust the interpreter's adherence to confidentiality rather than the therapist's.

Clients who have refused an interpreter despite limited English have fed back that they would not trust an interpreter to keep the information confidential outside of the session. Individuals have described how they would feel embarrassed or ashamed of discussing private thoughts and feelings in front of two people, one being from the same community and potentially representing the perceived values of this community to a client.

It can be important to remember that in some languages it is possible to offer an interpreter who speaks a client's language but is not from the same country. Often this can provide some reassurance to clients who fear and anticipate judgement or simply require, as a client once described to me, *some distance from home*.

The therapist starting the session by emphasizing the confidentiality of the interpreter and the service can be immediately reassuring. Ask the client to speak only two sentences at a time and explain that the interpreter is committed to capturing everything that is being said in the way it has been said. Be prepared to stop clients if they are speaking for too long as they adjust to the rhythm.

Do not expect the interpreter to pace the narrative. It is stressful for an interpreter to be left listening to long streams of dialogue, not knowing when the client will stop, and feeling anxious that not everything disclosed will be remembered. If this occurs, the interpreter inevitably has to summarize what is disclosed without reflecting the emphasis within the narrative. Under duress, they may lose focus and forget some meaningful details.

Therapists should speak in a normal tone and in the first person. Do not give the interpreter responsibility to ask the client a question, as this transforms the conversation from a direct dialogue between the client and therapist into a broken narrative, and creates a dynamic where the interpreter becomes an advocate or intermediary.

The therapist should aim to approach the session in the usual way and be authentic. It is important for the therapist not to alter his or her language except to be culturally sensitive and accessible. Avoid jargon, and try not to use words that do not exist in the language of the client and interpreter. If the therapist states, 'You seem depressed', and there is no word for this, the interpreter may well try to define depression from his or her own perspective. Interpreters should not be left to explain specific words or phrases, either from the dominant culture or from therapy and mental health terminology.

When therapists are seeking to understand a client's despair, or are concerned that a client is depressed, it is helpful to describe the set of feelings and behaviours associated with mental health distress rather than use medical terminology. It is important to minimize the use of mental health jargon, which may alienate clients and may make some individuals fearful of the stigma attached to it.

For refugees in exile, it can be an opportunity for the therapist to explain some of the commonly used words of the mental health field that may have baffled a client in contact with other health services.

For refugee clients, the context of therapy has the potential to offer some insight into the new world around them. Give explanations, and assume no shared understandings. The interpreter is likely to be uplifted and encouraged by the clarity with which you express yourself and relieved to know that he or she is not left feeling responsible or shouldering the responsibility for helping the client understand what therapy is. Gurris reflects how the therapist can become a representative of the host/asylum country for many refugees and so a therapist's role can be 'to educate patients about this alien culture in a manner that is enlightening, sensitive and neither injurious or condescending' (Graessner et al., 2001: 41).

After ten minutes or so, check that the client fully understands the interpreter. Sadly, there have been occasions when clients have responded that communication is fine out of politeness or for fear of losing much needed support or the session ending prematurely. Clients who have had to wait several months or longer for an appointment may feel under particular pressure to ensure that the session continues. Clients may feed back that communication is fine out of respect for the position of the interpreter who is older than them or perhaps because they are intimidated by the position of power the interpreter holds. The interpreter could also indicate that the communication is going well, despite evidence to the contrary – that is, constant checking of words and meaning between client and interpreter.

Trust your instincts and be prepared to ask the interpreter to leave the room so that fluency in communication can be checked. During a first session with a young Sudanese woman, an Arabic interpreter was booked who was new to the service. There was an uncertainty in the client's face at the beginning of the session and she seemed to be concentrating on the interpreter's every word. Despite the therapist's best efforts to be clear, a lot of time appeared to be spent in seeking clarification from the client by the interpreter and she could see the client begin to withdraw.

The therapist reflected to the client that she was aware that communication was not straightforward and requested that the interpreter leave the room. She asked the client if she could understand her in very basic English; the client nodded and said she spoke *a little bit* of English. The therapist apologized for the interpreter not being suited to her needs, and they arranged to see each other the following week. A different Arabic interpreter was booked, this time from Sudan. When they met again, the client and therapist were able to discuss the interpreting difficulty in the previous session and were able to progress their work together. The first interpreter's accent had been so different to anything she had heard before that she had really struggled to understand what was being said to her.

It is both the therapist's and the interpreter's responsibility to ensure that communication is clear. A professional interpreter will say immediately if communication is poor. However, in some circumstances, interpreters will feel a pressure to somehow translate in a very basic way what is said by one or both parties. On such occasions, it is the therapist's role to stop the session and discuss how the individuals in the triad are communicating. If therapists notice that the English of the interpreter does not reflect the subtleties of their exchanges with the client, therapists also have the right to change interpreters so they too can express themselves freely.

Be explicit about what therapy is, and be prepared to give time to explaining how therapy might help, to an individual new to the UK or new to therapy in general. Therapy is a Western construct and so it is helpful for the therapist to describe in some detail how therapists can assist individuals in distress and what clients can expect as therapy progresses. 'The methods which people use to maintain their psychological equilibrium and to find help are, in large part, developed and defined by the cultural, societal and health rules and meanings these are ascribed in their "world"' (Tribe, 1999: 569).

Be prepared for clients to focus their attention on the interpreter for some time in the early stages of the therapeutic process. Patience is really important; it is only when clients feel secure about the interpretation and in their relationship with the interpreter that they can fully focus on the therapist. A study by Miller and colleagues on the role of interpreters in psychological therapy with refugees found that it was common for clients to initially form a stronger attachment to the interpreter than the therapist. It was noted that once the relationship between interpreter and client was established, clients were then able to build a therapeutic alliance with their therapist (2005).

There will be occasions when there is an easy and straightforward start to therapy and psychological contact between client and therapist occurs quickly. If this happens, be aware that such an immediate connection that excludes the interpreter might not mean the client feels immediately safe with the therapist, but is an indicator of the client not feeling safe with the interpreter.

If a client asks a direct question of the interpreter, the therapist should explain that it is policy for interpreters not to answer direct questions. As with any direct personal question asked of a therapist, it is important to explore what might lie behind the question. One example between a therapist and a Kurdish survivor of torture from Iran illustrates this well. It was clear that the client had a concern about the interpreter in the assessment and tried to resolve this by probing him.

The crisis service had booked a Farsi interpreter for a male client from Iran. The service had very little information about this client – just that he had been tortured and was from Iran. The client was new to the therapist and he appeared reserved, even suspicious, when they first met in the waiting room. Once everyone was seated, the client looked even more hostile and the therapist observed that he was trying to gauge the attitude of the interpreter, who was a gentle and unassuming presence.

He asked the interpreter, 'Which part of Iran are you from?' The interpreter just translated the question back to the therapist.

The therapist responded, 'I understand why you might ask that question but Ali is here to interpret and so is not able to answer personal questions'. The response may have been too formal and the client seemed immediately silenced; and so a dialogue was opened up by the therapist.

Without exploring his questions and concerns, there was a risk of creating an environment whereby the therapist held an authoritarian position in the triad. The interpreter would have been positioned as a distant and inflexible translator who was present but not known and perhaps also representing authority.

At this stage the survivor said that he could not 'trust anyone' from his country after 'what had been done to us'. It became clear that he was Kurdish, a fact that had not been stated on the referral form. The therapist was then able to offer him the choice of having a Kurdish Sorani interpreter. He remained very polite and said that the interpreter was fine. The therapist reiterated that it was straightforward to book a different interpreter next time and reflected that in her experience, most Kurds she had worked with preferred to work in Kurdish. She explained that the interpreter would fully understand this and not be offended. He again said it was 'fine' and was respectful to the interpreter, smiling at him reassuringly. However, he remained distant for the rest of the session and she felt sure that further dialogue was needed with a Kurdish interpreter. She was also concerned that without intervention, he was unlikely to return.

The following day, she rang the client with a Kurdish interpreter, and he was able to request to continue with this same Kurdish interpreter used on the phone. Her efforts to ensure he was comfortable meant they engaged well in the second session.

A valuable lesson was learnt; often behind a personal question to an interpreter lies a concern. Therapists should trust their instincts and follow up with a client if they are worried that the interpreter has compromised an individual's sense of safety in therapy or made a client feel uncomfortable.

The client later explained that it would not have been culturally acceptable for him to refuse the first interpreter's presence as it would have felt rude, and created additional challenges for him personally. He wanted to work in his first language and, despite the gentle presence of the Farsi interpreter and the therapy agency's knowledge of the interpreter's political commitment to support Kurdish clients, he felt as if the oppressor was in the room. It would have inhibited his expression, affected his safety and created some complex internal struggles that could negatively affected his ability to use therapy.

He later shared how overwhelmed he felt at the initial assessment and what a huge effort it would take him at his lowest ebb to reach these two individuals so different from him. He felt as if no one could ever understand him and the thought of trying to talk to these two strangers was exhausting. He remarked how when the therapist and the Kurdish interpreter sat with him at the next session, and they seemed to know each other, it enabled him to feel closer to the therapist. He sensed that she must have had some understanding of the Kurdish struggle because she had recognized why it was so important to him. He said that he started to trust that therapy 'might be possible' when he saw them both seated together, whereas before he had felt ambivalent.

When working with a dissociative client or a client who has frequent flashbacks, ensure that the interpreter has been briefed on trauma and understands how the therapist will support a client. In some narrative trauma work, therapists are endeavouring to support an individual to revisit traumatic memories in a managed process. The therapist will use the present tense to re-visit a memory, ensuring the client does not lose connection with the present. The past tense is used to separate what was being felt then from what is being felt now. 'It is vital that the interpreter understands what the therapist is doing and relays their questions and the clients answers in the correct tense' (Boyles et al., 2015: 15).

In EMDR and some other trauma models, there is specific language recommended for use when processing traumatic memories. Preparation with the interpreter and consideration of such language are crucial if the therapist is going to be effective. The language of EMDR is so precise that we have found that practising particular phrases and words is a vital part of preparation for the interpreter.

On one occasion with an interpreter new to the service, a client jumped up in an assessment session and rushed to a corner of the room, crying out. The interpreter looked very alarmed and was now sitting on the edge of her seat. The therapist told the client (and therefore the interpreter) what she was doing in terms of responding to the flashback. She reminded the client who was in the room that she was in the therapy in the UK and that she was safe. She was wholly aware at the time that some of what she was saying was for the benefit of the interpreter. She repeated that everybody was safe, gently grounding the client using sensory awareness grounding skills.

As the client appeared less disorientated, the therapist gently raised her hand to the interpreter to encourage her to sit back from the edge of her seat and indicated that she should slow down her interpretation. Her calm and slow voice was being interpreted back, fast and anxiously. As the interpreter began to feel more contained, she began to follow the therapist's lead, and they were both able to support the client to return to the present and then orientate her.

During any crisis or critical incident when there is an interpreter present, there may be a temptation for the therapist to leave the room and seek support from colleagues, leaving the client and interpreter alone together. The therapist should ask the interpreter to get help if it is required, and remain with the client. If the therapist does have to leave the room, then both the therapist and the interpreter should leave together. Therapists should first explain to clients their reasons for doing this and ensure clients are not made to feel that they are unsafe individuals, or be left wondering why the interpreter is not prepared to remain in a room alone with them.

There may be silences in therapy and these can often be uncomfortable for clients of course, but interpreters can find them difficult too. Untrained interpreters may attempt to fill the space by repeating the previous question or reflection, or look expectantly at either the therapist or the client. Managing silence is a useful area to explore in the briefing. It is important to describe to interpreters what you expect of them during silences but also why they might occur and why silences can be helpful. Interpreters are far more likely to work hard at managing silence if they know their worth. Ask interpreters to sit back a little, look down but not drop their head as it may appear as if they are embarrassed. Advise interpreters not to say anything or look towards the therapist or the client. Ask the interpreter to leave it to the therapist or the client to break the silence.

This is a skill that my co-writer has fully developed and there have been times when Nathalie seems more comfortable in the silence than many therapists!

For interpreters, silences are a puzzle at first. They are mainly used in dynamic settings with time constraints, and have to process the maximum amount of information as quickly as possible. Pauses and silences are disconcerting, and interpreters may even wonder whether the client is unhappy with the translation or has lost trust in them.

Interpreters can register and process information at a phenomenal speed. When a client pauses to reflect for an indefinite amount of time, interpreters can lose momentum and be tempted to worry and question their own performance. It can be challenging for someone who is used to dealing with words, memorizing and rendering them accurately without stopping, to suddenly find him- or herself faced with this space in a setting that is usually filled with language. This should not be more than a passing moment, and an ethical interpreter instinctively respects a silence, sensing that it plays a key part in a conversation and has a therapeutic value.

Interpreters learn to become comfortable with silences and welcome them as enriching, giving more texture to words and thoughts, and as a breathing space that can bring humanity and cohesion. Interpreters begin to value listening to the silences, getting into a mood and understanding these moments like pauses in music. Silences are a time for reflecting and putting words together or a safe time to face sad memories and name them. A pause can be a moment that allows clients to safely anchor themselves in their thoughts, take the lead and regain power over their memories.

So how does one interpret silence when there are no words to work with? What new meaning will the silence bring into the following words spoken by clients when they decide to resume the conversation with the therapist? Interpreters will learn not to break a silence. They will remain alert and not disconnect or use the pause as a recreational space in which to run through their own thoughts, or even relax a little. There is too much at stake. They listen to silence as attentively as they listen to words. An interpreter may even adapt their breathing to the client's, to be in unison and prepare themselves for the next piece of dialogue to interpret.

Listen for responses from the client that indicate that the reflections the therapist is making or the questions being asked are being altered or softened by the interpreter. As a therapist builds a trusting and collegial partnership with an interpreter, the interpreter becomes a subtle and gentle presence that a therapist rarely acknowledges or considers in the session. However, in the early days of working together, it is good for the therapist to be aware of the temptation interpreters might have to change what is being said. This might be because an interpreter is concerned that the therapist is crossing a cultural taboo, or because it triggers an emotional response in him or her, or perhaps a judgement is being made about the therapist's reflection or intervention.

Challenging any distortion of a therapist's words is important. It can be helpful to say that there has been a misunderstanding, and wonder if the question asked has been translated clearly and ask the question again; 'you mentioned that you were thinking about suicide a lot, and I wanted to ask you about whether you had made a plan to harm yourself'. In this instance, the interpreter might be steering away from interpreting the frequently asked questions of a suicide risk assessment as he or she is shocked or uncomfortable at the directness of the question. Providing a briefing on the process of a suicide risk assessment will ensure that the interpreter is fully engaged in accurately reflecting your questions during a risk assessment.

Be aware of a client who appears watchful of the interpreter; a French-speaking client who watched the interpreter throughout the session would often answer the therapist in very broken English or correct the interpreter, as if she did not trust the interpretation. She seemed anxious and the therapist could see her attention was focused on ensuring her words were being translated properly.

If clients appear to be overly concentrating on the interpreter's translation or they correct or clarify frequently, it may be that the client has identified that the interpreter is not accurate, or is not fully focused or engaged. Find an opportunity to check with clients about whether they are happy with the interpreter and show your commitment to getting the right fit.

Like therapists, interpreters have limitations and are not always performing at their best, especially on a busy day, when concentration is affected after several assignments without a break. We have both known occasions when clients have noticed a difference in the rendering of their narrative and have alerted interpreters in order to ask them to refocus. If managed thoughtfully and in an environment of trust, this can be empowering for clients, who want their voice attended to and their rights respected. Such moments can have an equalizing effect and deepen the relationships in the triad.

An Iranian Christian convert recently remarked to the interpreter that he knew she was fasting and suspected that was why she had clarified the same sentence several times! It was a warm and affectionate challenge, and the first time he had acknowledged her directly in the session since the early days of their work together.

Good practice guidelines for therapists in working with interpreters:

- Speak in the first person, with your normal tone and speed.
- Be yourself; a good interpreter will aim to capture the essence of how a therapist expresses him- or herself, as well as capture the client's style of expression.

- Fully brief and prepare the interpreter for the session, describing the therapeutic approach/structure of the session and what the interpreter can expect in terms of support.
- Do not interrupt the interpreter or respond in the client's language if you also have some knowledge of the language as this can interrupt the flow of communication and be very confusing for the interpreter and client.
- Speak just 1–2 sentences at any time and ask the client to do the same; gently pause a client speaking for too long to reduce the pressure on the interpreter.
- Sit directly opposite the client, and your eye contact should always be with the client, not the interpreter.
- Do not leave the client on his or her own with the interpreter.
- Never say anything to the interpreter that you do not want interpreted for the client, and avoid any direct conversations with the interpreter.
- Be thoughtful around the use of proverbs, metaphors and myths. Often cultures may share similar sayings and the telling of these can create powerful connections across cultures.
- Intervene if a client asks any direct questions to the interpreter, to ensure the interpreter does not feel obliged to answer.
- Intervene if the client passes a visual recording, picture or document to the interpreter and consider the needs of the interpreter if a client wishes you to look at an injury or scars.
- If the interpreter appears to be having a conversation with a client, challenge this in the session and remind the interpreter to translate all that is being said.
- Be prepared to terminate a session if you are concerned that the interpreter is not interpreting all that is being said or if the client appears anxious and unsafe in the interpreter's presence or does not understand the dialogue. The session can also be terminated if the therapist is unhappy with the attitude or approach of the interpreter.
- It is the therapist's responsibility to manage the session, and unless it is likely to undermine a client, it is acceptable to challenge the interpreter if he or she is leading the session in any way.
- It is good practice to try to use an interpreter who is not known to the client from other professional settings, to preserve the unique space of therapy.
- Do not use children or family/community members or untrained interpreters to interpret in a therapy setting.
- It can be helpful to pause after 20 minutes in a first session to check communication is clear.

- Trust your instincts; if you feel that your words or emphasis have been altered, where possible, challenge immediately unless it might be harmful to the client. This will model to the client that you expect accurate communication and he or she has a right to professional interpretation.
- Ensure that the confidentiality policies of both the interpreting agency and therapy service have been fully understood by the client.
- Be prepared to book a different interpreter in the future, accepting that miscommunication amounts to denying an individual the resources to properly communicate and prevents therapists from being able to practice to the best of their ability.
- Interpreters should be asked to keep their mobile on silent.
- Ask interpreters to keep their mobile out of sight, as some clients may be concerned that the interpreter may be recording on a phone during the session.

5 Debriefing the interpreter

There is a growing recognition about the mental health impact on interpreters of working within the psychological therapy field (Miller et al., 2005). However, most freelance and agency interpreters are not offered supervision and many are not debriefed after sessions with healthcare professionals, including therapists.

Interpreters in supervision groups have described how frequently they have walked into settings with disturbed and angry clients and had not been prepared for the material they were exposed to. They also report not being debriefed after difficult sessions. Interpreters can leave one challenging session and go straight into another, with no break or acknowledgement of the potential impact each session has had.

Debriefing should be offered after every therapy session, and most therapists offer ten minutes immediately after the client has left the room. If for some reason, a session overruns and an interpreter is not debriefed, it is good practice to meet before the next session, or offer an alternative debriefing slot.

The role of the debriefing session is twofold. It is an opportunity to offer support to interpreters after a difficult session and enable them to reflect on the impact of the work. It also enables both the interpreter and the therapist to improve their working relationship and discuss any difficulties that occurred in the session, or clarify any misunderstandings. It can also be a time for the interpreter to offer some cultural knowledge, or for the therapist to share in more detail how he or she works, or prepare the interpreter for a change in direction or pace.

Its primary focus, however, should be to provide support. Interpreters are profoundly affected by the material they hear. It is important to remember that the interpreter hears the narrative first, and then has to voice over very difficult material, reflecting the tone of the client, without losing composure or showing facial expressions. Interpreters have their own life experiences. They can feel distressed and saddened by the experiences of their clients, and what they hear can trigger difficult memories and unresolved issues. They may be concerned or confused at their responses to a client or about emerging dynamics in the room.

Sometimes interpreters' complex emotional reactions can be alarming to them and there will be a need to examine their responses more deeply. Both the interpreter and therapist may need to assess what needs to be put in place to ensure the interpreter is kept psychologically safe and able to sustain the work healthily. "Therapists must be attuned to the impact of an account which may raise powerful feelings, some painfully repressed, in the interpreter especially if the interpreters have, in their time, been refugees too' (Dearnley, 2000: 20)

Therapists working within bereavement or hospice settings where clients are facing serious illness or their own death should be aware of the support needs of interpreters due to the often profound impact of this type of work.

A therapist had been working in a setting with a Kurdish Sorani interpreter whom she knew well and had a positive working relationship with. In a session, the interpreter had been dipping her voice when the client swore and raised his voice. The client was very aware of the interpreter and although his focus was directly on the therapist in the sessions, he would sometimes examine the interpreter as she translated his swearing. The therapist noticed that when the interpreter was with this client, she would sometimes put a pillow over her stomach and the therapist wondered whether it offered some form of protection as the client was often angry.

The debriefing enabled the therapist to feed this back to the interpreter and she was able to share how uncomfortable she felt at his language. She also recognized that he had noticed her voice dropping when he swore and was becoming curious about his impact on her, which was distracting from the work together.

After the discussion, the therapist noticed that she tried hard to reflect his language and tone and was more relaxed in sessions. The debriefing provided an opportunity for her to explore how it felt to say such swear words. In the therapist's clinical supervision, she was able to reflect upon why he potentially might be provoking her in this way. The supervision dialogues were taken back into the debriefings and both therapist and interpreter continued to reflect on his changing use of language throughout their work together. The initial debriefing had challenged her to reflect his tone, but also provided support and encouragement to continue. Furthermore, she was given a choice about whether she felt able to sustain working with him. The long-term and trusting partnership led to both the interpreter and therapist being very collegial in their approach. Managing this dynamic in the triad deepened their working relationship and provided learning for both in their future work together.

When therapists establish a team of trusted interpreters and can develop such helpful partnerships, there can be genuine excitement at some of the dialogues in the debriefing. Working relationships can form that create a hugely containing and productive therapeutic space for clients. This particular interpreter went on to undertake a Certificate in Counselling course to enhance her interpreting skills in our therapy setting, a sign of her commitment to building on her expertise.

On many occasions, the reassuring presence of an interpreter who shares the same language culture and/or country of origin has allowed some clients to introduce themes into therapy that they may have struggled to name had an interpreter not been in the session. Raval's study illustrated that practitioners felt that clients were able to share their cultural or religious beliefs when an interpreter was present (1996). Raval reflects how therapists report that 'their work is enhanced by the interpreter helping them develop a better cultural understanding about the service user, helping them gain greater communication and engagement with the service user and helping them obtain accurate information about the service user' (2003: 21).

The purpose of debriefing:

- Provides an opportunity for interpreters to reflect on how they feel after the session and express any concerns.
- Provides an opportunity for interpreters to give the therapist feedback or share any challenges they experienced in the session.
- Provides an opportunity for the therapist to give feedback on the interpreter's good practice, but also indicate what could be improved or share any areas where there were concerns.
- Enables both to assess whether interpreters have recovered from a difficult session and have not been impacted to such an extent that they require more support from the therapist/agency.
- Enables both to assess whether the impact of the ongoing work requires additional 1:1 supervision.
- Provides an opportunity to assess whether the therapist's approach is fully understandable to the interpreter, and clarify any misunderstandings.
- Assess whether further training is required for a new approach – for example the therapist using EMDR.
- Provides support and encouragement to sustain difficult or complex work.
- Provides an opportunity to check any concerns or doubts the therapist might have about any element of the interpretation – for example the client said he felt like he was 'never going to be free'. The therapist is not sure whether he meant free of his memories or free from the asylum

process. The interpreter might not know or may have been clear but assumed the therapist understood the context.

- Provides an opportunity for interpreters to share their understanding of the meaning of what has been said on a cultural level, and this may include providing an interpretation of non-verbal communication.

6 Managing challenging dynamics

There will always be challenging dynamics that occur in the triad. Some may be about language or misunderstandings about meanings or gestures; others may be cultural or related to the global structures of power and the positioning of the individuals involved in the triad. In settings where clients and interpreters are from the same country, 'It is important to be mindful of the way in which power differentials originating in the country of origin may affect the relationship between psychologist, interpreter and client, particularly in the light of political and social conflict' (Tribe and Thompson, 2008: 3). The most common dilemmas or dynamics we have experienced in our work together are explored further ahead.

In most cases, the debriefing enables an opportunity to explore dynamics that have occurred in an appointment. Sometimes the therapist may decide to open up a dialogue about the dynamic in the next therapy session. Often therapists will take interpreting dilemmas to clinical supervision prior to exploring them with an interpreter. Therapists may at times struggle to make sense of the way in which an interpreter and client are relating to each other. Commonly they may find themselves feeling excluded in the three-way relationship, or have concerns about how attached the interpreter is to the client. As a good working relationship builds between the therapist and interpreter, such dilemmas can be resolved between you and often be explored in the triad.

> If we can adjust our positions very slightly and foster a greater knowledge and awareness of each person's role and expectations, we can minimise the parts of us which exist 'outside' the relationship, minimise the 'cliquing' of twos within the three, and give ourselves the largest platform of communication on which to engage.
>
> (Smith, 2008: 22)

In some settings having access to joint supervision may be a helpful option if there are complex dynamics, or splitting in the triad that requires further exploration. Joint training can create meaningful dialogue that can assist in existing and future working alliances. 'The closeness of clinician and therapist and their space to reflect jointly are the elements that can be used to manage and negotiate any pulls in the three-way relationship' (Tribe, 2009: 21).

A key lesson from our work together as therapists and interpreters has been to address difficulties as soon as they arise and not to retain an interpreter if the therapist senses that the dynamic is not working. It is common for therapists to struggle along with an interpreter they have concerns about longer than is necessary. Clients who do not have English as a first language are often in a variety of settings where they struggle to access services with qualified interpreters. Tolerating a three-way relationship that is not containing or helpful to the client risks denying an individual genuine access to therapy. Therapists have an ethical duty to ensure that individuals can fully communicate, and so any dynamic with the interpreter that blocks a client's ability to use therapy or inhibits a therapist's ability to practice safely must be addressed.

Clients often do not feel able to complain about an interpreter, especially if they have a shared cultural background. However, the therapist *is* in a position to voice a concern and has the power to respond.

Often it is only when the usual interpreter is on holiday and a different interpreter is booked that the therapist gains some insight into the impact. When the change occurs, the client may not be different with the new interpreter, but the therapist becomes aware that they have found an interpreter who seems fully engaged with their therapeutic approach, enabling them to be more effective as a practitioner.

A frequent challenge is when the client and interpreter have worked together in a previous professional setting. If a client requests his or her 'usual' interpreter or there is just one interpreter for a language in the town or region, the therapist may have to manage this delicate dynamic. The interpreter and client enter therapy with an established relationship, and the interpreter has considerable power as he or she is likely to know significant details about the client that are not known to the therapist. This can impact on how the therapist and client engage. However, in many instances, it may also mean that engagement happens quickly, as the client already knows and trusts a member of the triad.

Therapists should ensure that the client is aware that they will have no access to any of the material known by the interpreter. Professional interpreters will separate what they know from past professional contacts from what is shared in therapy. Inevitably, no matter how committed and boundaried both the interpreter and therapist are, the reality is that the client will remain aware of what the interpreter knows and what the therapist does not know. This may result in a sense of confusion in the clinical setting that inhibits how helpful therapy can be. Clients may choose, as is their right, not to disclose a pregnancy or a rape in therapy, but remain aware that the interpreter knows this information – from a GP appointment for example. Clarity and close adherence to boundaries and confidentiality are vital here, but the impact on the client can still be significant.

There are times when the alliance between the therapist and interpreter is too close, and this in itself can feel excluding. When interpreters are working hard to be professional and boundaried, they may appear too separate and clients may feel overwhelmed by the power of the two professionals in the room, finding no point of connection to either individual.

Clients may feel betrayed, expecting the interpreter to immediately represent them in some way as a member of their 'community' and feel confused when the interpreter appears distant or positions him- or herself as having some form of authority. Interpreters themselves have shared that when they 'have been' in the same difficult place as a client, they have sometimes misjudged how much professional distance to create in order to protect themselves from past memories of seeking help at a time of need.

The sense of powerlessness many refugees feel in professional settings can remind refugee interpreters of situations where they too have struggled to have a voice, or relied upon an interpreter. For some interpreters, the difficult experience of seeking asylum may be quite recent and so they create an emotional distance that is experienced as rejection or pity by a client. This is particularly the case for individuals seeking asylum who are living in poverty or are destitute. The sense of hopelessness and the day-to-day struggle of destitution can create a profound sense of despair and humiliation. At such times, professional and well-dressed interpreters can reinforce a client's sense of failure and humiliation.

A common dynamic as therapy starts is the engagement between the interpreter and client, often felt by the therapist as excluding. To some extent this is inevitable as both client and interpreter share a language and/or a culture. Clients may also think that they share with the interpreter common experiences too, such as the position of being in exile, or experiences of racism in the UK.

In our experience, African clients may often refer to their interpreter as a brother or sister and make a connection that can be felt by a non-African therapist immediately. Where the therapist is African but does not speak the language of the client, the powerful bond of language still creates an immediate connection between the client and interpreter.

Therapists new to using an interpreter need to be patient and secure in their ability to engage with clients. They also have to wait for trust to build and the attention to gradually move away from the interpreter, before reverting to the primary relationship between the therapist and client. Interpreters can assist this process by giving less eye contact once their relationship with a client is established, and keeping their head dipped in concentration. This can encourage a shift in focus in the therapy room.

Interpreters can struggle to separate or adjust to the emerging relationship between the client and therapist. They may disengage slightly when trust is established between therapist and client, as they feel less important. This may be due to the interpreter's own need to feel connected and useful. The conversations to address this in the debriefing need to be carefully managed, but are worthwhile and usually helpful in the long term to the interpreter. Many interpreters will understand and enjoy the client and therapist's engagement as it forms. Others may perceive therapists as insecure when they try to address an interpreter's over-attachment to a client.

Interpreters are very aware that their work may be of a transient nature, whether it is performed in a long-term contract or in briefer work. They appreciate that they are likely to withdraw when clients choose to express themselves in English. They take great care at rendering the client's narrative and they will sense whether a client can follow their translation.

An experienced interpreter cares about striking a delicate balance in the therapy room, aiming to preserve a feeling of privacy between the therapist and client. This is a subtle task and one that it is hard to find words to describe, but is apparent in our work together. Nathalie is present, but there are times when my closeness and contact with a client can feel just between us. These moments of intimacy are witnessed by Nathalie, but she does not intrude upon them or simply just observe them.

There may be occasions when interpreters feel that they are intruding in the relationship between the therapist and client, or feel uncomfortable about the intensity of the dialogues. The intimacy and the slow pace of a therapeutic setting can be destabilizing to an interpreter used to more business-like sessions.

Interpreters may take time to adjust to the boundaries of therapy as they are frequently given too many responsibilities by other professionals; a GP might ask them to accompany a patient to the pharmacy, or an asylum lawyer could request that they sit with a tearful client after a witness statement and offer moral support. In a therapy setting, interpreters need to find their moorings and read a new map. It is usually a surprise but also a relief for interpreters to discover that they are not expected to cross a threshold, but it may not be obvious to them at first and they may come across as unboundaried or unskilled.

Interpreters will move from an assertive to a reflective mode of interpreting quickly if fully briefed and will come to enjoy the therapy process. As an interpreter, I enjoy and learn from watching how different therapists work in our current setting. I never cease to be amazed by all the diverse and yet very structured gentle communication strategies that are being deployed by the therapist. The task of interpreting becomes a complex task as we listen attentively to reflections, and become more tuned to small nuances that can make such a difference to the therapist's work.

A challenge for interpreters is rendering a sense of humour. Some humorous remarks translate well within cultures, but many do not. Interpreters may be prepared for a client to joke but have difficulty keeping composure and refraining from smiling or responding before they interpret it back to the therapist.

In a way, laughter from the client is more challenging than a silence, as it is by nature infectious and a moment of connection as well as a communication in itself. It requires more discipline from the interpreter as it is often spontaneous. It can be more challenging to appropriately interpret for a therapist engaging in a humorous exchange with a client. Interpreters are never sure whether this is the intent, and if they do not know the therapist well, they can be tempted to stay on safe ground, and play down the playfulness of the remarks. On such occasions, they are not sure if they have caught the intention correctly, as often these moments of humorous connection can be subtle.

A therapist was working with an Afghani survivor who would often make jokes in sessions to distance himself from his pain, and as he was very funny, this could be a distraction for both the therapist and interpreter! Whenever he joked, the interpreter would spontaneously laugh before he even had time to interpret the survivor's words. The therapist wanted to smile and acknowledge the humour but she also wanted to ensure that he could continue to express his distress. The immediate connection between the client and interpreter when he joked excluded her for a few seconds, but also actually impaired her ability to practice. It took several sessions for the interpreter to understand how the warm smiles and laughter between him and the client might be impacting on relationships in the triad as well as preventing the client from staying with painful feelings. As the sessions progressed, the interpreter could see for himself how the client was using humour to avoid his feelings.

The client was reassured that he could make both the interpreter and therapist laugh, and had retained this side of himself despite the horror he had survived, but a balance needed to be found. The shared humour between the interpreter and client slowed down the survivor's use of the therapeutic hour as he would launch into funny stories at the start of the session as it clearly brought pleasure to the interpreter. Sharing a sense of humour with the interpreter as a first interlocutor also brought in a connivance and the impression that they could understand each other without having to spell things out, and unwillingly put the therapist at the remote end of the triad.

The impact of any informal and friendly contact between the client and interpreter has the potential to stall therapy. If this had gone unchallenged, the risk may have been that the interpreter and client continued to build a close alliance, where the relative relief of warm and funny observational stories blocked the therapeutic work. The situation could have led to the client associating the therapist with pain and distress, and the interpreter with comfort and friendliness. It might also have led the client to wonder whether the therapist was a necessary intrusion as the closeness between the interpreter and him developed.

There will be times when the material or the levels of distress in the room impact on interpreters to such an extent that they are overwhelmed in the session. Often interpreters have their own experience of persecution, war, torture or abuse, and so it is likely that their past traumatic experiences will be triggered by the material being voiced over. Therapists will need to be alert to the interpreter's needs when undertaking work with trauma and abuse. If an interpreter's voice wavers or if the therapist begins to sense the interpreter is overwhelmed, it can be helpful to suggest that the interpreter take a break and pause the session.

Our experience is that clients will usually understand that the interpreter is upset. However, care needs to be taken to ensure that clients understand the interpreter is being supported, and that they are not to blame or responsible for causing distress – that is, that it is normal for interpreters to be moved and affected. Often it can be reframed as a reflection of an interpreter's compassion towards a client.

In situations where interpreters are overly impacted, consideration will need to be given as to whether it is appropriate to continue and whether the interpreter should withdraw. In some situations, we can be overprotective of both clients and interpreters and it is enough just to acknowledge that the interpreter is moved without over-examining the impact on the client. In the same way that a therapist appearing visibly saddened by a client's experience can be therapeutic, the same response from an interpreter can have therapeutic benefit too.

Therapists frequently express concern that when they deliver a long reflection or show gentle curiosity about a particular issue a client is describing they hear what sounds like a short firm sentence delivered in a questioning manner by the interpreter. The client then responds by giving a brief answer. The therapist suspects that his or her reflection has been turned into a statement or a question. Our advice would be to show curiosity about the change in tone or for the therapist to reflect that there may have been a misunderstanding. Often is it not the intent of the interpreter to change the emphasis, or it may be that the therapist has not understood a language issue. Either way, asking questions about interpretation may enable clients to challenge or question the interpreter, or seek clarity when they are unsure that the meaning of what they have said has been conveyed.

Challenging or questioning the interpreter in front of a client could be experienced as destabilizing or could create anxiety about making mistakes. If cultural mores are crossed in such challenges, it can be empowering for clients, but can also be uncomfortable and alienate both the client and the interpreter.

A therapist gently asked an African survivor through a Lingala interpreter why she felt her brothers had arranged for her to come to the UK following her imprisonment. During her detention in the DRC, she had become pregnant following a rape. The question was carefully framed as the therapist sensed that there were difficulties around her brothers. The survivor had said when therapy first started how wonderful her brothers were. However, the therapist noticed that she seemed distant and unsure when she talked about them in more recent sessions. She would often use language such as 'sent me away', appearing angry and distressed. In early sessions, she had used phrases such as 'helped me escape', 'risked everything for me' or 'saved me'.

The therapist's two rather long sentences seemed to be delivered in one short punchy sentence, and her reply was 'they got me out of the country because I wasn't safe, I told you when I first came' [to therapy]. The therapist reflected that she felt that there had been a miscommunication and asked whether she could repeat her question; the interpreter delivered the question again. The client went very quiet; 'it is hard as I sometimes wonder if they sent me here not to protect me but because I brought them shame'. The survivor went on to explore her concerns and the therapist sensed that the interpreter shifted in terms of her concentration.

In the debriefing, the therapist explained that she was concerned that she had asked a difficult question very carefully but the interpreter had been very brief in her delivery of it, and it sounded as if it had been interpreted as a direct question. The interpreter was initially defensive but eventually acknowledged that she had attempted to clarify why the client's brothers had sent her away as she felt herself it was not clear. It gave the therapist an opportunity to re-visit the importance of reflecting her tone, translating the meaning of what she said at all times and never seeking to clarify or seek answers to her own questions.

Sitting with unanswered questions or fragments of narrative can of course be a real challenge to an interpreter, whose natural inclination is to try to make a sentence easy to understand when it might be jumbled and confused.

Asking interpreters to ensure they transfer repeated phrases and confused sentences is a common theme, and interpreters will develop their skills in this if supported and encouraged. Interpreters may have been criticized previously for translating hesitations or repeated words in non-therapy settings and may take great pride in their proficiency and language skills. They may be tempted to edit the client's syntax and expression, even upgrading a few words, for cultural reasons or because they are trying to improve the quality of communication.

The sharing of cultural understanding with the therapist can be helpful, but can also carry risks. It can be challenging if an interpreter has strong views about a culture and its cultural norms and unintentionally or not brings those expectations into the clinical space.

In therapy with lesbian and gay clients, we have always endeavoured to be gay-affirmative in our approach, in that our 'beliefs and values appreciate homosexuality – and bisexuality – as valid and rich orientations in their own right' (Davies, 1996: 40). Therapists should ensure that interpreters working with lesbians and gay men are gay-affirmative, and ensure that attitudes around sexual minorities are explored in the briefing.

An interpreter working in a refugee setting described herself as 'quite traditional' in some of her opinions. Although the therapist and interpreter disagreed on many issues, the therapist never felt this impacted on the therapeutic work, or could be sensed by clients. The client was a lesbian and had recently arrived in the UK. The therapist had discussed at length with the interpreter the gay-affirmative approach in the service to working with lesbians and gay men, and the interpreter had previously worked alongside lesbian and gay therapists during her time at the service.

In the briefing session, the interpreter said that she knew that lesbian and gay sexuality was looked upon differently in the UK and she was 'non-judgemental'. Her position of tolerance felt uncomfortable and so a number of dialogues about adopting a gay-affirmative approach were had before therapy started. The therapist entered the three-way relationship with some reservations about the attitudes of the interpreter.

The client had a strong lesbian identity and had been an activist around lesbian and gay rights in her country. She was grieving for her losses and angry at the killing of her partner prior to her moving to the UK. She appeared watchful at times of the interpreter but had quickly established a good therapeutic alliance with the therapist, and the therapist felt the relationship between the client and interpreter was good enough. When the client was exploring an aspect of her imprisonment, the therapist made a reflection, and the client's response seemed slightly out of step. The therapist felt concerned and wondered if the interpreter was missing some of what the client was saying because she found it difficult to say.

This was addressed in the debriefing with the interpreter and she was able to describe what aspects of the material she was finding uncomfortable. Once she had voiced this and understood its potential impact on our client, she was able to interpret the client's feelings about the loss of her relationship.

The interpreter was positively and inherently challenged by the work with this young woman and personally changed as a result. The danger of course would have been that the client had sensed this homophobia, and it could have caused psychological harm and affected the safety and containment of the therapeutic relationship. She could have felt the same sense of judgement emanating from the interpreter that she had experienced in her country. A failure of the therapist to challenge this may have almost replicated past experiences in the torturing state of the authorities failing to protect her from homophobia and, when she sought help, being further harmed.

The interpreter can be an ally if he or she is well informed and prepared for interpreting in settings where clients are either highly distressed or agitated and confrontational. Interpreters should always reflect the tone and physicality of the therapist and the client. The occasion where this differs is when the client is very angry and shouting, and there is a risk of the client harming him- or herself, the interpreter or the therapist.

When working with an angry and potentially aggressive client, the interpreter adopting the same pitch and tone of the client could aggravate a potentially risky situation. The therapist is trying to calm the client, and will be adopting common de-escalation techniques that may diffuse an individual's anger. It is evident to the therapist that the client is shouting, and so on these occasions, interpreters should reflect the tone of the therapist only, but ensure that they translate everything that is being said, including swear words and threats, as this will enable the therapist to assess the level of risk.

In the same way, if a client is having a flashback and shouting or screaming, the therapist can clearly hear this and needs to know only the content of what is being said. The therapist's aim is to ground the client and use a calm and gentle voice that the interpreter will need to reflect. On such occasions there may be more eye contact and other non-verbal communication between the therapist and interpreter to reassure the interpreter and follow the distress of the client. The interpreter may need the therapist to see his or her anxiety and the therapist may need to indicate, non-verbally, that everyone is safe.

We have at times experienced a dynamic when a client is holding negative feelings towards an interpreter, perhaps due to the client's own prejudices or assumptions about an interpreter's identity or background. Interpreters may feel a low level of hostility in session, but not share it with the therapist, trying to remain impartial and professional. Encouraging interpreters to share their hunches with the therapist in the debriefing session enables a therapist to support the interpreter and may mean exploring the dynamic in therapy at some stage if it is affecting therapeutic work.

A therapist and a French interpreter were working with an African woman who was well educated and an experienced lawyer. She had been imprisoned and tortured for campaigning for women's rights in her country. She made a special connection with the therapist, as they shared a similar political framework. The client trusted the therapist and approached her about writing a report on her mental health to support her claim for asylum.

Her asylum lawyer had instructed a psychiatrist from a different agency to write a report, but the client was reluctant to re-visit painful memories with a stranger, and hoped her therapist would write it instead. The therapist carefully explained that the client should discuss this with her legal representative, and chose not to intervene or advocate for the client. The client was shocked at the refusal and her demeanour changed dramatically. She looked cold and distant, turned away from the therapist and leaned towards the interpreter, engaging in strong eye contact and visibly excluding the therapist. Her sense of anger and frustration was palpable. The interpreter was concerned that she had resorted to an alliance with her because she felt betrayed, but she also understood that there was more to it.

Culturally, asking for help from an individual who has a position of power is not easy and being refused is even more difficult. It may have been cathartic for her to voice her disappointment at that moment, but the upbringing she had received was preventing her from doing this. She was trying to remain composed, despite her shock and anger. The interpreter gently pulled back in her seat to add a symbolic distance, and engaged in just a little eye contact. She remained present and attentive to both individuals (who mattered to her) and stayed carefully in her position, despite the pull from the client.

In the debriefing, the therapist reassured the interpreter and confirmed that she had respected the balance in the triad. Both practitioners explored the impact of the therapist's refusal on the client and the issues of power and culture that were present. It took some time before the client grew to trust the therapist again, and the interpreter had to be careful in those next few sessions, as the client clearly felt a strong alliance with her, and her sense of betrayal continued for some time.

Tips for the therapist in handling challenging dynamics:

- Trust your instincts and use the debriefing to raise any concerns about the session, or to challenge the interpreter about a particular response.
- If there has been a misunderstanding in the room or the therapist or the client has been misinterpreted, seek clarification during the session.

- If communication is becoming difficult, stop the session and address it.
- If the therapist has concerns about the interpreter's attitudes, address in the debriefing and offer further training if there is a willingness to learn and reflect.
- The dynamics occurring in the session may be related to the therapist showing a lack of cultural sensitivity and resulting in a deepening of alliance between the interpreter and client, and/or alienating a client. The debriefing can be an opportunity for the interpreter to share cultural information and express such concerns.

7 Managing shifting power dynamics in the triad

There can be a variety of factors that influence the shifting dynamic of power in the three-way relationship and there are likely to be many occasions where the dynamics are highly complex. The dynamic may reflect the structural positions and/or experiences of oppression of the three individuals in the room or even link back to, or mirror, family relationships. They may also relate to recent experiences of conflict or to the position of power of the individuals in communities. Tribe advises having a wide lens when trying to understand what might be taking place in the triad (2009).

Themes of power are ever present in work with people seeking asylum in the UK and survivors of torture and organized violence. In the West there is considerable anti-immigration and xenophobic rhetoric directed towards those who seek asylum in the UK. Alongside this, the Islamophobia on the rise in Europe and the United States means that many survivors of any form of persecution or abuse will carry a fear of racism, or harm, by the authorities into the therapy room. Survivors may dread or expect racism or prejudice from the therapist and/or agency or judgement by an interpreter. Clients may feel that they need to prove themselves to be 'genuine' to both professionals in order to have a right to their support and understanding.

The therapist and interpreter should aim to practice anti-oppressively and be aware at all times of how they might impact on another. Many therapists will aim to work self-reflexively. Self-reflexivity is an important feature of practising ethically as it requires the practitioner to consider as they practise, moment to moment, how their position, reactions and assumptions influence their responses. 'Working with an interpreter requires a greater degree of self-reflexivity on the part of the practitioner, as different levels of relationship and communication need to be understood' (Mudarikiri, 2003: 185).

Despite a therapist's intention to be client-centred and collaborative, 'the therapist generally adopts the privileged position at the apex of the triangle, controlling the literal choice of language used in therapy (usually English), the therapeutic context, the choice and use of psychological technologies and perhaps the direction of change' (Patel, 2003: 223–224).

A therapist was working with an Iranian man who had held a high-profile position in his country. The interpreter was a highly qualified and middle-class linguist, whose interpretation was competent, but he always felt slightly aloof in terms of his presence. The therapist had been concerned that although he understood therapy, he was not wholly respectful of it. However, he sat quietly with distress and she did not feel he was uncomfortable with the anguish and despair brought to sessions by clients.

The client held views about women's position in society that were challenging for the therapist. She had always suspected that the interpreter held similar views but knew such views could not be expressed in the setting both worked in. When the client became animated during one session, he began to express anger at his wife's growing independence but also said some personal and direct comments about the therapist and her appearance.

His voice was raised and he talked of her freedom and said that he did not want his children to have the sort of 'freedom' she had. The therapist noticed the interpreter became more animated at this point and the exchange felt difficult. The therapist and client were eventually able to explore his loss and how deskilled and disempowered he felt in this new society. He was able to explore how even within his own home, he now no longer held the power he once had.

The therapist suspected that she may have got to these painful explorations quicker with a different interpreter and perhaps even been able to explore the impact on him of being vulnerable and assisted by a younger white woman who he felt did not understand or respect his position. The sense of joint outrage being felt and expressed by both men meant he retained his anger for a significant part of the session as it was subtly fuelled by the interpreter. He became increasingly agitated, despite his obvious distress.

The therapist sensed that the interpreter and client were closely positioned, and at times in the session, it felt as if they were almost speaking as one. She was intimidated and at several points became anxious. She glanced towards the interpreter at one stage as she had never heard him so animated; his face was flushed, and he seemed to have grown physically and was leaning forward in his chair. He was fully engaged in a way that was unfamiliar to her.

The debriefing and subsequent 1:1 meeting between the therapist and the interpreter were difficult and they agreed to stop working together. Alongside the themes of gender, race and culture, there was also an issue about the age of the therapist; she was younger than both men. The issue of class was equally present, as both men were highly privileged. The therapist was aware from clinical supervision themes that the internal struggle she experienced during the encounter may have been fuelled by her own awareness of her limited use of language and the fact that she had not accessed further education. This issue had often surfaced within her therapeutic work with well-educated clients in the past. She certainly had to work hard to assert herself in meetings with this interpreter, and noticed his use of language grew more sophisticated when they discussed their differences.

At any time, the global structural positions in society of each person in the room in terms of race, gender, class, age, disability and sexuality, and other oppressions will result in some complex dynamics. In most settings, clients can feel as if they have little power in terms of their position as clients in receipt of, and potentially dependant on, a service. Westermeyer reflects that the 'three roles of clinician, interpreter and patient are not the same in terms of professional, legal or symbolic status. Although the patient can "hire or fire" the other two, there exists the imposing physical fact of two staff against one patient' (1990: 747).

Raval argues that the 'power differential and the inequality between the clinician and the service user becomes greater when there are differences in language and culture, and the service user is disadvantaged by not being able to speak the dominant language of the host country' (2003: 10).

The mental health and therapy field continues to evolve and has developed intercultural or cross-cultural approaches and transcultural psychiatry (Fernando, 2001). Alongside this, therapists continue to develop anti-oppressive practices in their work, aiming to 'find unique and meaningful ways to hear our clients' voices that do not deny them power and replicate discriminatory experiences' (Bains, 2010: 23).

Anti-oppressive practice in the triad:

- Ensure that the interpreter and therapist keep a dialogue open in the debriefing around the shifting power dynamics in the room.
- Remain alert to the potential of both the interpreter and/or therapist replicating a client's experience of oppression, and ensure that the briefing creates an opportunity for a dialogue around themes such as working from a gay-affirmative approach or with class awareness.
- Ensure that such dynamics are explored where possible in therapy.
- Therapists working in non-refugee settings may need to be overt in their support of the rights of those who seek asylum in the UK when working with refugee clients.
- Avoid using the language of the therapy field, which is likely to be unfamiliar or excluding to many clients, especially refugees or those seeking asylum in the UK who are new to therapy as a form of support and where there may be taboos around mental health as well as different help-seeking norms.

8 Support and supervision of the interpreter

In addition to debriefing after every session, we would recommend that interpreters practising regularly in a therapy setting should have access to supervision by a therapist. A supervision group can be a powerful and helpful space as it allows the facilitation of mutual support and learning between interpreters and creates a team that can support each other within their day-to-day work. It is useful for this to be facilitated by one or two therapists, either from the agency or from another therapy service working with interpreters. The frequency should be at least bimonthly, and more if this is possible.

Providing ongoing continuing professional development in the form of training will also ensure that your interpreting team can continue to build on their skills and expertise. Inviting the interpreting team to events and briefings within the service enables interpreters to feel part of the team and its culture and has the potential to build strong working relationships.

When systems change or a new approach to therapy is introduced into the team's delivery, offer training to the interpreting team to enable them to build confidence about this new approach. It can also be helpful to run joint interpreter/therapist training days to look at common themes and dilemmas in the work.

If an interpreter is finding the nature of the material or working with a particular client overwhelming and distressing, interpreters should be invited to explore whether particular client work is not suited to them. At other times, the intensity of the work being undertaken has meant that 1:1 supervision is necessary in order to protect and support an interpreter to continue undertaking highly charged and difficult work. There have been many occasions in our mutual work with survivors of torture where it has been entirely justified for the interpreter to have regular 1:1 supervision. This has ensured that an interpreter is able to process the content of the session, can reflect on his or her self-care and is educated about vicarious trauma. Therapists can also share tools for managing distress and impact.

Therapists have a duty to protect their interpreters, and many interpreters may well find it hard to say that they cannot continue out of a sense of duty and commitment to the client. The experiences of our clients can often trigger therapists, who may have had similar life events, whether they too are a refugee or a survivor of some form of abuse or trauma. Therapists have training to manage such material being triggered, and have often had or are in therapy. Interpreters have rarely had access to such training and their first experience of the process of therapy is as a professional through an interpreting assignment.

Debriefing and supervision might seem unfamiliar to many interpreters, but most will use this space well if supported and encouraged. What can feel uncomfortable for many interpreters in this setting is when they too feel like they have become a client, and the debriefing or supervision session has led them into exploring personal themes with the therapist that they have not planned to discuss. The intimacy of the partnership can be powerful, and it is important that therapists are mindful of interpreters' need to keep themselves safe, retain their privacy or be appropriately defended during difficult work.

Supervision can also be a time to support interpreters in maintaining boundaries, which are constantly challenged in long-term therapy, especially in services where interpreters may frequently bump into clients in the course of their work in the building.

There are occasions during therapy when interpreters can feel unsafe and be unclear about how to manage boundaries in a given situation. The boundary of the interpreting role is very similar to that of the therapist in that interpreters too are required not to engage in relationships or friendships with clients. They are also not allowed to share information about themselves. In long-term work, however, it is almost inevitable that the client will be curious and there may be instances when the therapist makes a personal disclosure, and it could be helpful if the interpreter also shares some information with a client.

At any time, interpreters are seen as experts, community representatives, potential friends and advocates by clients. Among such expectations, it can be hard for interpreters to be clear about their boundaries when the two people they are working with may not fully understand their position and role. Supervision offers an opportunity for therapist and interpreter to fully explore the expectations that might be placed on the interpreter by the client and how the therapist might assist in making roles clearer.

Support and supervision of the interpreter:

- Interpreters should be offered a pre-briefing when starting to interpret for a new client or when working with a therapist for the first time, allowing the therapist to share his or her approach.
- Interpreters should always be debriefed after a session and offered further support or supervision sessions if the interpreter is overwhelmed by a client or the material.
- Interpreters benefit from ongoing group or 1:1 supervision as well as ongoing continuing professional development.
- Interpreters benefit from having access to self-care training and education about vicarious trauma and other impact responses, such as compassion fatigue.
- Therapists should give interpreters a break after 50–60 minutes and check that the interpreter is resourced for the next session.
- Giving interpreters a separate space in the service acknowledges the complexity of their endeavour and ensures they have a preparation and recovery space.

9 Ending the three-way relationship at closure of therapy

As therapeutic work draws to a close, the ending between the client and interpreter will need to be built into planning for the closure of therapy. In long-term work with refugees who are learning English, therapy with the interpreter being present may end after the therapist and client have agreed to work in English.

However, in many situations, the ending of the three-way relationship happens at closure. For clients, losing the triad can be doubly painful as no longer having the validation of two people can be regarded as a significant loss. This loss is amplified if the client is a refugee with few sources of support in the UK.

In most therapeutic contexts, the interpreter does not have his or her own voice in therapy sessions, and never speaks directly to the client or therapist unless to seek clarification. The ending session is the one time that most therapists familiar to working with interpreters will facilitate the interpreter being able to speak directly to the client. The therapist will also give the client an opportunity to respond directly to the interpreter. As a therapist, I will also speak directly to interpreters to say my good-byes and to thank them for their contribution to the therapy, as well as acknowledge the ending of the triad.

Ending sessions are by their very nature often painful processes for clients, and can be particularly so for refugee clients, for whom loss and separation are key themes. Interpreters have often been impacted by the therapeutic work and are keen to have permission to acknowledge their feelings towards the client and to wish them well. They may also want to share that they too will miss the three-way relationship. The interpreter may want to discuss what happens if client and interpreter bump into each other in the community afterwards, and reassure the client that his or her confidentiality will be retained beyond therapy.

Clients often feel a profound wrench at the loss of the interpreter and are keen to thank them and say good-bye, but sometimes also wish to continue some form of social contact or friendship. It is really important to ensure that the interpreter and therapist prepare for the ending session so that the interpreter can explain why this is not possible, and the therapist will support and be involved in this carefully managed exchange.

The words of the interpreter to the client should be said in the client's language first, and then in English so the therapist stays included; and the same process applies when the client talks directly to the interpreter. It may appear confusing and unusual to change the dynamic, and make provisions for the interpreter to have his or her own voice, but the client often has something meaningful to say to the interpreter. Clients often feed back how important the interpreter's role has been, and reflect on the meaning of his or her presence throughout the duration of therapy, and how that might have changed.

Sometimes therapists can underestimate the depth of the relationship between client and interpreter and not arrange for a final ending session of the three-way dynamic. This can leave both the client and interpreter with unresolved feelings and concerns. In most cultures, it is very important to thank a person who has assisted you at a time of need and failing to do this can feel profoundly uncomfortable. Even in short-term work, where the alliances may not have developed to the same degree, ensuring that you provide a space for everyone to say good-bye and have discussed what happens when you meet away from the clinical setting is vital.

Therapists working in brief settings may neglect to give the end of the triad its due significance. At these times, clients may miss the therapist, but they may retain some feelings for the interpreter that go beyond the professional relationship. They may perceive the interpreter as a brother or like a mother or sister, and acutely miss the familiar presence of someone who knows and shares their cultural framework. Clients often ask us if they can retain a friendship with interpreters outside of our service, and find it painful when the boundary of the interpreting role is applied.

To a lesser extent, but still of importance, it should not be forgotten that interpreters also have a relationship with the therapist. The partnership is safely contained within professional boundaries, but interpreters translate for therapists too and develop esteem and care for them. Ending a counselling contract equally means an ending of all relationships in the triad.

Managing the closure of the triad:

- In both short- and longer-term work, ensuring that there is an opportunity to end the three-way relationship is important and it may be the only occasion when the three individuals in the triad speak directly to each other to say good-bye and explore the meaning of their work together.

- If the therapy is going to continue in English, always ensure that the three-way relationship has an ending or closure.
- It is important to discuss and prepare the client for bumping into the interpreter in the community or public sphere, and to explore how the client might want to respond, reiterating confidentiality.
- The client should be told that interpreters cannot initiate contact if they meet outside of the professional setting, but can respond if the client initiates it.
- Prepare interpreters for this shift in the session when good-byes are said, so they have time to prepare their words as it can be unfamiliar for interpreters to have their own voice.

10 Interpreting on the phone or via Skype

There are significant limitations in working with an interpreter on the phone for therapy, and if possible it should be avoided unless this is the only option available to the therapist. Telephone interpretation 'suits simple tasks, but complex or sensitive communications are best left to in-person interpretation services, where non-verbal cues are an important part of the communication process' (Smith, 2008: 22).

In phone interpreting, the same key principles and guidelines apply in that the phone interpreter should have access to briefing and debriefing. In my practice, telephone interpretation is used solely for short clinical calls and not for therapy, with the exceptions of support given to refugee clients held in an Immigration Removal Centre (IRC) in the UK.

If resources allow, hands-free calls are preferable as the client can hear the voice of both the therapist and the interpreter throughout the exchange.

Avoid where you can the interpreter holding the phone, as the client and interpreter are more likely to feel as if they are speaking directly to each other and the interpreter is not protected from the force of the material. We have found that speaking a little slower in this context can be helpful. If a hands-free device is not available, sitting in close proximity so that the client can hear the therapist's voice in the distance is a compromise. Never ask interpreters to dial the number themselves as clients may be anxious that interpreters have their telephone number. When ending the conversation, ensure that it is the therapist who is that last person to say good-bye to a client.

For clients who are concerned about confidentiality, telephone sessions do offer a greater sense of privacy. However, the inevitable curiosity the client may have about the interpreter is harder to address or resolve when only the interpreter's voice can be heard. It can also be challenging for the interpreter to convey the meaning of what is said without the visual cues and personal knowledge of both the client and the therapist.

Clients often harbour fears about the judgements of unknown interpreters on the phone as they cannot read body language for clues. This can also feel disconcerting for therapists as they worry that there are attitudinal responses that they cannot sense through body language, facial expression or tone. Therapists often feel less able to build a close working alliance with the interpreter or to offer genuine support after the session.

Skype is preferable to telephone interpreting and, although challenging, offers the possibility of eye contact and, for rare languages, facilitates access to interpreters all over the country. The seating has similarities – that is, the therapist faces the client, and the client can see both the interpreter and the therapist via the screen. The interpreter can also see both individuals.

The therapist and the interpreter tend to be seated nearly side by side in the beginning. However, after the usual introductions, the therapist and interpreter may agree that the interpreter can sit further away, to enable the therapist and client to more fully engage. This allows the therapist to have more direct eye contact with the client, and gives the interpreter the opportunity to take notes if needed. It is good practice for interpreters to ask permission to take notes and the client should be informed that the notes will be shredded by the interpreter after the session.

Communication on Skype can feel strange to interpreters and they may feel more exposed. They may be tempted to edit some of the narrative, as they can regard Skype as a more business-like vehicle, and so may endeavour to prioritize clarity over capturing the expression of a client.

Telephone and Skype interpreting:

- Try to use hands-free devices for phone calls so that the client can hear both the therapist's voice and the interpreter's voice at all times.
- Speak a little slower than your normal speed for telephone interpreting.
- The same briefing and debriefing guidelines apply.
- The same rules of impartiality and confidentiality apply.
- In a Skype setting, similar seating can be created as face-to-face sessions.
- In both situations, note taking is allowed. The interpreter hands the notes back to the therapist at the end of the conversation, or in a Skype setting the client should be informed that notes will be shredded.
- Always introduce yourself first on the phone as the therapist, and hand the phone over to the interpreter if unable to use a hands-free device. The client will understand that the therapist is the only one who has access to his or her telephone number.
- When ending the conversation, the therapist should be the last person to say good-bye to the client. Most clients can understand simple greetings in English.

11 Working with children and young people

In our experience, the impact on the interpreter of working with children and young people can be considerable, and the pull to abandon or loosen boundaries harder to resist. Children and young people can quickly become attached to the interpreter in the absence of their own family and can often see the interpreter as a family member. At other times, young people can be overwhelmed with the two adults in the room and struggle to find their voice.

The impact on the interpreter can be amplified if the child or young person is an unaccompanied asylum-seeking child without the presence of a parent or guardian or a trafficked young person at risk of further exploitation. The definition given by the Home Office is a person under 18 years of age or who appears to be under that age. Children in this situation are also referred to as separated young people or unaccompanied minors.

Children and young people's attachment to their language may be complex. Costa writes, 'The tension between the old and the new, the language of the heart and the head, can have a huge impact on asylum-seeking and refugee children' (2016: 6).

Keen to fit in and adjust and often learning English quickly, they can lose their original first and second languages and later feel considerable loss as they settle and search for an identity in the host country. Individuals can find it difficult to find a place in either their own or the host culture, and loss of language can form part of that struggle.

In therapy, careful consideration needs to be given to what language young people would like to work in. Assumptions should not be made that if a young person speaks good English, then therapy in English should be the choice of language used in therapy.

Working with children and young people:

- Careful exploration of what language to use in therapy is important, even though it is common for young people and children to learn English quickly.

- Consideration should be given as to whether the interpreter responds to direct requests from children in therapy, such as asking the interpreter to pass them a figure from a sand tray. Flexibility is needed here, and planning between therapist and interpreter is essential.
- Debriefing is essential, and often additional supervision is required to support the interpreter to maintain boundaries and resist the temptation to protect or parent a vulnerable young person. This tension may be amplified for interpreters who share a culture with the child or young person.
- When using art, sand play or other forms of creative therapies, such as psychodrama, briefing interpreters on how they might manage looking at pictures or activity in the sand tray will be important. There are no hard rules here, but an agreed way of managing these dialogues is vital.

12 Interpreters in couple and family therapy

Increasingly systemic family therapists and relationship therapists are adapting their approach to include an interpreter in the room. It is vital that the interpreter is seen as an integral member of the team and his or her role respected and supported. Due to the complexity of family work, allowing more time for briefing and debriefing is important. In our experience, it can be challenging for interpreters to resist aligning themselves to individual family members, and interpreters often describe situations where they find themselves becoming part of the family dynamic.

Interpreters, as in other settings, may have useful information to share with the systemic team about culture, child- and family-rearing approaches and roles in the family's country of origin.

In family therapy or couple therapy, the interpreter is usually in the circle, and equidistant from each family member. The therapist's focus will still be on the clients in the room, and not the interpreter. Therapists usually arrange the seating so that no member of the family has priority over the others, including children and young people. The nature of couple and family therapy is that the therapist is likely to be interacting with everyone in the room throughout the session. In some settings, there may be two therapists, or a reflecting team. As in the three-way relationship in individual therapy, a rhythm will develop once everyone settles into a comfortable group communication.

It can be a very pressurized environment for interpreters, however, as they endeavour to interpret for three people or more. When there are children, it can be more challenging, as children move around the room, play and interact. In a fast-moving family therapy environment, interpreters will adapt well to the pace, but therapists need to be mindful of the pressure it can put on them. Interpreters have to earn the trust of all members of the family, ensuring they express each person's narrative accurately.

It is important to plan how interpreters indicate which client they are interpreting for in a fast-moving dialogue. We have seen different styles at work here; some interpreters will say the first name of the person they are interpreting for before translating, and others will gently indicate with a gesture who they are interpreting for.

The interpreter has to be aware of the family dynamics in the therapy, and the power struggles that may be present. The debriefing is vital in helping the interpreter and therapist work effectively in this complex setting, ensuring that the interpreter is attentive to all family members.

Many of the families that interpreters are working with, certainly in refugee therapy settings, may be families who are reuniting after many years apart. Those members of the family who have recently arrived into exile are adjusting to a partner who may be a very different individual from the one they knew before being separated. The potential for the new arrival/s to feel overwhelmed or overpowered in this setting is considerable. It will be both the interpreter and the therapist's role to remain mindful of this and ensure that they are not lost or disempowered in the process of family therapy.

Those family members who are new to the UK will not be familiar with a helping agency's involvement in their family; 'the interpreter needs not only linguistic skills, but also an awareness of these processes so they operate within themselves and in all parties in the room so that families can feel understood and accepted' (Loshak, 2003:152). The same writer goes on to reflect that above all families need 'emotional contact with professionals who can move freely and comfortably across cultural boundaries themselves and bear to listen to painful experiences. The interpreter's own skills, knowledge and capacity for empathy are crucial to such contact being effective' (152).

In our experience, often the newly arrived refugees are likely to be the mother and children. Women may not be used to voicing opinions in public, or will be uncomfortable if they are seen to disagree with their partners. They will be profoundly unfamiliar with having the privacy of the family setting witnessed by others. In some cases, women may defer to their husbands in session and it may take time for this dynamic to change and for all those in the room to have a voice. From our experience, women have often sat back in early sessions and have not always fully participated in the conversations taking place. We have seen how initially women will observe how the professional female interpreter from their country operates on an equal footing with the professional therapist, and this can be both empowering and unsettling.

Where an interpreter communicates with a therapist with ease, it is more likely that the family will be more inclined to experience the therapist not as an expert but as someone to confide in and trust. In this way, the interpreter can assist in a family's engagement with the family therapy team and help build trust and a collaborative approach to future work. In family therapy settings where the potential for alliances is considerable, the sense of containment a skilled and empathic interpreter can bring is significant.

'Relationships within refugee families undergo radical transformation and role reversals are not uncommon' (Papadopoulos, 2002: 36). Following a long period of separation, women may arrive in the UK to join a partner after having become independent in their home country. Once reunited, women may find their role in the family has changed, and find their partner depressed and disturbed following torture and/or defeated after a long and agonizing journey through the asylum process.

Interpreting in couple and family therapy:

- Take time to outline how the interpreter/s will work together in a family setting with all family members when you first meet, ensuring time is taken to explain the interpreter's role to everyone present.
- Be aware of possible tensions around differences in class, culture, race, age, religion and so forth between the family and the interpreter.
- In a family setting, the interpreter is not responsible for managing the flow of communication, but can feel pressure to do so when there is fast-flowing dialogue.
- Discussion between the interpreter and therapist prior to family work is essential so that there is agreement about whether the interpreter responds to requests from children – for example to look at a drawing or pass a figure from the doll's house.
- In a fast-moving family dynamic, children may speak to themselves during play. It will be important to agree that all narrative is interpreted, however inconsequential it may seem to the interpreter. A skilled interpreter may often interpret the dialogues of older members of the family, but gently indicate or gesture to the child playing in the sand tray, and interpret the child's narrative too.
- In large families, consider having two interpreters to reduce the pressure on the interpreter and ensure that all family dialogues are captured.
- Children often learn to speak English before their parent/s and may understand the questions or reflections of the therapist/s. This may mean they respond before the interpreter has had the opportunity to interpret, and this can create some confusion. Yong people and children will learn to wait if supported by the therapist, but the interpreter should not be left to manage this without support.
- In family settings, non-verbal communication between the interpreter and therapist occurs automatically as the pace of the dialogue requires this.
- Agree how interpreters will indicate which family member they are interpreting for, either by naming the client before interpreting or by a subtle gesture towards the client.

13 Interpreters in a therapy group setting

It can be helpful to have two interpreters for groups of eight and above. Most therapy groups are usually for 1.5 hours and the amount of interpretation involved can make it extremely challenging for one interpreter. If just one interpreter is used, it can be hard to sustain the required level of concentration for the duration of the group and ensure that all dialogue is captured.

Planning is key between the group therapists and the interpreter/s, as well as establishing clear ground rules with group members at the beginning. It is important for group therapists to explore how to work with the two interpreters with clients at the first group meeting, to reduce confusion and miscommunication. Depending on whether the group is mixed in terms of gender, it can be useful for the interpreters to reflect the gender mix of the group.

There is often a range of accents and levels of education in a group setting and these expose themes of power and privilege. When there are dynamics in the group that directly reflect structural experiences of oppression, interpreters will need to ensure that they share their observations with the therapist/s after each group.

An interpreter fed back that in a French-speaking men's group, one of the clients had not had access to an education in his country of origin. The rest of the group had been educated in French and had been fairly privileged in their home countries. The group therapists had little French and had not identified the significant differences in the French being spoken in the group, or realized that this individual's voice was disappearing as he struggled to manage his sense of inferiority in the room.

Without the interpreter's thoughtful feedback to the group therapists, this dynamic could have led to the client withdrawing from the group or being further oppressed and marginalized. The interpreter's feedback enabled these class differences to be named and explored in the group, and the individual was supported by the other men. He went on to gain considerably from the group experience despite his initial misgivings. 'Our socio-economic position, and consequent lifestyle, our values, attitudes and traditions and our life chances all impact on who we become and what we might bring to therapy' (Kearney, 2010: 115).

If there are two interpreters in a group, it is possible to agree with the group members and group therapists that each interpreter will take responsibility for particular individuals in the group. This arrangement enables the interpreters to deepen their understanding of those assigned group members and helps to ensure that meaning is more accurately conveyed as the interpreter's knowledge of each group member develops.

Interpreting in groups:

- In therapy groups of eight or more, use two interpreters to both reduce the stress on the interpreter and enable all dialogues and communication to be captured.
- At the start of group work, take time to agree together how interpreters will be used in the group.
- Group therapists will need to carefully manage communication as the group learns to work in two languages, and a flow begins to emerge.
- Interpreters frequently describe how challenging it can be to remain in role in a group setting, especially when the dialogue holds personal resonance and they feel a sense of belonging sometimes not felt in day-to-day life.
- In both group and family settings, non-verbal communication between the interpreter and therapist occurs automatically as the pace of the dialogue requires this.
- In group settings where there may be a range of accents, and clients have different levels of education, it can be extremely challenging for interpreters to capture the styles of communication in the group. Ensure that interpreters do not unwittingly expose those group members who have had little access to education. Our language reflects our privilege, and so careful consideration will need to be given to how such differences in the use of language are interpreted and their impact.
- Consider offering a half hour debriefing after group work to ensure the themes and complex dynamics arising in the work are fully explored.

Summary

Our years of working together have deepened our commitment to the belief that working in a triad can have a positive impact on clients and enhance the therapeutic endeavour.

I have often heard therapists report that there is a loss of emotional effect when an interpreter is present as it is the interpreter who witnesses first-hand and experiences the full emotional content of the narrative. My personal experience is the opposite. When the interpreter and I are aligned and we are all in psychological contact with each other, both the interpreter and I are impacted by the client's experiences. There have been times that I have wondered whether not knowing what is being said has enabled me to focus less on words and more on what I can feel and sense from a client. Perhaps it has made me more intuitive.

In addition, the repeating of a client's narrative in two languages may have a positive impact on individuals. A client may be able to sense what I am saying in my tone and affect, and even understand much of what I say as his or her English develops. My words are then translated and heard again in the client's chosen language, often with a subtle difference in emphasis. The impact of this can be significant in terms of bearing witness and processing traumatic and painful experiences and feelings.

I have found that working with interpreters has impacted on all aspects of my practice in a positive way. In the past, I often assumed I understood the meaning of what was being said when there was a shared culture. Now I rely neither on my own understanding nor on the interpreter's; I ask what a client means, and I ask this all the time. Pearce uses the term 'cosmopolitan communication', in that we are all shaped by culture and our own history and background, and our understanding or way of finding meaning in the world is not superior (1989). 'Nothing is taken for granted about each individual's unique way of seeing the world, their values or their use of language, and each person's world-view is accorded equal status with our own' (Messent, 2003: 149).

In my working experience as a therapist, interpreters have enabled me to work in a more profound way with an individual and have deepened my relationship with a client, rather than detracted from it. When seated at closure, clients have described how important it has been to speak in their chosen language or reflected that they have been able to freely express themselves when speaking in their mother tongue. However fluently any individual speaks a language, we know that to say any particular words at any given moment in our first language can often mean only one thing, and often its meaning is impossible to translate. This is indeed the nature and beauty of language; it is not just words.

A phrase loaded with cultural and personal context can feel impossible to explain to anyone who does not share the language or culture, and loses both its power and meaning when we endeavour to explain it. When exhaling loudly the other day with my team, I said the phrase 'I'm losing the will'. I was immediately understood and was greeted with knowing smiles and supportive laughter. It was said with humour, and I was clearly not expressing a genuine loss of hope but expressing a momentary frustration at a bureaucratic process. The meaning was clear, and it was the ironic use of an emotive phrase that was understood by all present. That same day, I said to a client on the phone, 'Feel free to ring me when you have left'. He went quiet and said, 'I am not free'.

In therapy, clients should not have to search for words within a limited vocabulary or have to simplify sentences or lose tense and subtlety. Individuals should be able to speak with the full meaning of what has been said being fully understood, especially at times of distress and emotional or personal confusion.

It is our clients' right to have freedom of expression, and one way in which a therapist can secure this right is to do all we can to engage qualified and professional interpreters, who are appropriately prepared and supported to undertake this work.

References

Amnesty International. (2006) *In-Depth Study on All Forms of Violence against Women: Report of the Secretary General*. UN General Assembly. A/61/122/Add.1,6.

Bains, S. (2010) Racism as a Trauma. In: Lago, C. and Smith, B. (eds) *Anti-Discriminatory Practice in Counselling and Psychotherapy*. London: SAGE (pp. 23–32).

Baker, R. and Briggs, J. (1975) Working with Interpreters in Social Work Practice. *Australian Social Work* 28(4): 31–37.

Bakhtin, M. (1981) *The Dialogic Imagination – Four Essays* (ed) Michael Holquist, Trans. Caryl Emerson and Michael Holquist. Austin: University of Texas Press.

Boyles, J., Talbot, N. and Pahlevan, B. (2015) We Cannot Talk If We Do Not Feel Free. *Therapy Today* 26(8): 12–17.

Costa, B. (2011) When Three Is Not a Crowd: Professional Preparation for Interpreters Working with Therapists. *ITI Bulletin* January–February: 20–21. www.ethnologue.com.

Costa, B. (2016) Language Matters to a Refugee Child. *Therapy Today* 27(8): 6–7.

Crawford, A. (2012) Court Interpreter Checks Non-Existent. *BBC News, UK*. 9 August.

D'Ardenne, P., Ruaro, L., Cestari, L., Fakhoury, W. and Priebe, S. (2007) Does Interpreter-Mediated CBT with Traumatised Refugee People Work? A Comparison of Patient Outcomes in East London. *Behavioural and Cognitive Psychotherapy Journal* 35:1–9.

Davies, D. (1996) Towards a Model of Gay-Affirmative Therapy. In: Davies, D. and Neal, C. (eds) *Pink Therapy: A Guide for Counsellors and Therapists Working with Lesbian, Gay and Bisexual Clients*. Buckingham: Open University Press (pp. 24–40).

Dearnley, B. (2000) Psychotherapy in Translation, One Clinicians Experience of Working with Interpreters. *Society of Psychoanalytical Marital Psychotherapy Bulletin* 7: G12/022.

Fernando, S. (2001) *Mental Health, Race and Culture* (2nd edn). Basingstoke: Palgrave Macmillan.

Graessner, S., Gurris, N. and Pross, C. (2001) *At the Side of Torture Survivors: Treating a Terrible Assault on Human Dignity*. Baltimore: The Johns Hopkins University Press.

Herman, J.L. (1994) *Trauma and Recovery, from Domestic Abuse to Political Power*. London: Pandora Press.

Kearney, A. (2010) Class and Counselling. In: Lago, C. and Smith, B. (eds) *Anti-Discriminatory Practice in Counselling and Psychotherapy*. London: SAGE (pp. 115–124).

Loshak, R. (2003) The Role of the Interpreter in Child Mental Health: The Changing Landscape. In: Tribe, R. and Raval, H. (eds) *Working with Interpreters in Mental Health*. London: Routledge (pp. 151–167).

Messent, P. (2003) From Postman to Makers of Meaning: A Model for Collaborative Work between Clinicians and Interpreters. In: Tribe, R. and Raval, H. (eds) *Working with Interpreters in Mental Health*. London: Routledge (pp. 135–150).

Miller, K., Martell, Z., Pazdirekk, L., Caruth, M. and Lopez, D. (2005) The Role of Interpreters in Psychological Therapy with Refugees: An Exploratory Study. *American Journal of Orthopsychiatry* 75(1): 27–39.

Mothertongue. (2016) *Code of Practice and Ethics for Interpreters and Practitioners in Joint Work*. www.mothertongue.org.uk.

Mudarikiri, M.M. (2003) Working with the Interpreters in Adult Mental Health. In: Tribe, R. and Raval, H. (eds) *Working with Interpreters in Mental Health*. London: Routledge (pp. 182–197).

Papadopoulos, R.K. (2002) *Therapeutic Care for Refugees: No Place Like Home*. London: Karnac.

Patel, N. (2003) Speaking with the Silent: Addressing Issues of Disempowerment When Working with Refugee People. In: Tribe, R. and Raval, H. (eds) *Working with Interpreters in Mental Health*. London: Routledge (pp. 219–237).

Pearce, W. Barnett. (1989) *Communication and the Human Condition*. Carbondale, IL: Southern Illinois University Press.

Quevedo, G. (2010) Mapping Refugee and Migrant Communities in the UK. *ICAR Resource Guide*. September.

Raval, H. (1996) A Systemic Perspective on Working with Interpreters. *Clinical Child Psychology and Psychiatry* 1: 29–43.

Raval, H. (2003) An Overview of the Issues in the Work with Interpreters. In: Tribe, R. and Raval, H. (eds) *Working with Interpreters in Mental Health*. London: Routledge (pp. 8–29).

Scottish Translation, Interpreting and Communication Forum. (2004) *Good Practice Guidelines*. www.gov.scotgov.scot/publications/2004/02/18873/32914 13 Feb 2004/02 Scottish Executive, Scotland.

Smith, C.H. (2008) Bridging the Gap: Therapy through Interpreters. *Therapy Today* 19(6): 21–23.

Tribe, R. (1999) Bridging the Gap or Damning the Flow? Some Observations on Using Interpreters/Bicultural Workers When Working with Refugee Clients, Many of Whom Have Been Tortured. *British Journal of Medical Psychology* 72: 567–576.

Tribe, R. (2007) Working with Interpreters. *The Psychologist* 20(3): 159–161.

Tribe, R. and Thompson, K. (2008) *Working with Interpreters in Health Settings, Guidelines for Psychologists*. London: The British Psychological Society.

Tribe, R. and Thompson, K. (2009) Exploring the Three-Way Relationship in Therapeutic Work with Interpreters. *International Journal of Migration, Health and Social Care* 5(2): 13–21.

Van Parijs, P. (2004) Europe's Linguistic Challenge. *European Journal of Sociology* 45(1): 113–154.

Westermeyer, J. (1990) Working with an Interpreter in Psychiatric Assessment and Treatment. *Journal of Nervous and Mental Disease* 178(12): 745–749.

Wilson, R. (2002) *Improving the Health of Asylum Seekers in Northern Yorkshire: A Report on Service Provision and Needs*. Tandem. www.nypho.org.uk.

Index